BURSÁTIL

Dominar el arte de la creación de riqueza
a través de estrategias probadas y
técnicas probadas en el tiempo

Resumen: "El arte del mercado de valores" es una guía completa para dominar el mundo de la inversión y el comercio de acciones. Este libro cubre temas esenciales, incluida la comprensión del panorama del mercado de valores, las estrategias de selección de acciones, las técnicas avanzadas de negociación, la construcción de una cartera diversificada y el dominio de la psicología del mercado. También profundiza en conceptos más avanzados, como la sincronización del mercado, la inversión inteligente desde el punto de vista fiscal y la generación de ingresos pasivos. Si usted es un principiante o un inversor experimentado, este libro le proporcionará las herramientas y el conocimiento necesarios para lograr el éxito financiero en el mercado de valores.

Capítulo 1: Fundamentos para el éxito

1.1 Comprender el panorama del mercado de valores

El mercado de valores es un ecosistema complejo y dinámico, donde las empresas emiten acciones de su propiedad para ser compradas, vendidas y negociadas por los inversores. Estas transacciones tienen lugar en varias bolsas de todo el mundo, como la Bolsa de Nueva York (NYSE) y el NASDAQ. El panorama del mercado de valores puede ser intimidante para los principiantes, pero al dividirlo en sus componentes principales, se vuelve más fácil de entender.

Para entender el panorama bursátil, es esencial familiarizarse con los siguientes aspectos:

1. Participantes del mercado: El mercado de valores consiste en una variedad de jugadores, incluidos inversores individuales, inversores institucionales, fondos de cobertura y creadores de mercado. Estos participantes participan en la compra y venta de acciones, lo que afecta el sentimiento general del mercado y los movimientos de precios.

2. Intercambios: Las acciones se negocian en bolsas, que son plataformas que facilitan las transacciones entre compradores y vendedores. Las principales bolsas incluyen NYSE, NASDAQ, London Stock Exchange (LSE) y Tokyo Stock Exchange (TSE), entre otras.

3. Índices bursátiles: Los índices se crean para representar el rendimiento general de un mercado o sector en particular. Están compuestos por un grupo selecto de acciones que proporcionan una instantánea de las tendencias del mercado. Algunos índices bien conocidos incluyen el S&P 500, el Dow Jones Industrial Average (DJIA) y el NASDAQ Composite.

4. Capitalización de mercado: La capitalización de mercado, o capitalización de mercado, de una empresa se calcula multiplicando el número total de acciones en circulación por el precio de mercado actual por acción. Esta medida ayuda a los inversores a determinar el tamaño y el valor de una empresa, lo que puede ser útil para comparar empresas dentro de la misma industria.

5. Sectores e industrias de acciones: Las acciones a menudo se clasifican en sectores según la industria en la que opera la empresa. Los sectores comunes

incluyen tecnología, salud, finanzas, energía y bienes de consumo. Comprender estos sectores puede ayudarlo a diversificar su cartera e identificar posibles oportunidades de inversión.

6. Tickers y símbolos de acciones: Cada acción se identifica por un símbolo de cotización único, que es una serie de letras utilizadas para diferenciarla de otras acciones. Estos símbolos hacen que sea más fácil para los inversores y comerciantes rastrear y analizar las acciones.

Al familiarizarse con estos componentes clave del panorama del mercado de valores, estará mejor equipado para navegar por el mundo de la inversión y desarrollar una base sólida para el éxito.

1.2 Desarrollar una mentalidad ganadora

Para prosperar en el mercado de valores, es crucial desarrollar una mentalidad ganadora que le permita tomar decisiones bien informadas y mantenerse disciplinado a través de las fluctuaciones del mercado. Cultivar una mentalidad ganadora implica los siguientes principios clave:

1. Establezca objetivos claros: Establecer objetivos específicos, medibles, alcanzables, relevantes y con plazos limitados (SMART) es la base de una mentalidad ganadora. Estos objetivos le ayudan a mantenerse enfocado en sus objetivos de inversión y proporcionan un punto de referencia para medir su progreso. Asegúrese de revisar y ajustar periódicamente sus metas para reflejar sus circunstancias y prioridades cambiantes.

2. Adopte el aprendizaje continuo: El mercado de valores está en constante evolución y los inversores exitosos nunca dejan de aprender. Manténgase informado sobre las tendencias del mercado, las nuevas oportunidades de inversión y los cambios en el panorama económico. Esté abierto a aprender de sus errores y busque continuamente mejorar sus conocimientos y habilidades.

3. Desarrollar la inteligencia emocional: Invertir

en el mercado de valores puede ser una montaña rusa emocional. Desarrollar la inteligencia emocional le permite reconocer y manejar sus emociones, evitando que nublen su juicio. Aprende a mantener una perspectiva racional y evita decisiones impulsivas basadas en el miedo o la codicia.

4. Mantenga la disciplina: Una mentalidad ganadora requiere disciplina y consistencia en su enfoque de inversión. Apéguese a sus estrategias predeterminadas y pautas de gestión de riesgos, incluso cuando el mercado sea volátil o lo tiente a desviarse de su plan. La paciencia y la persistencia son esenciales para el éxito a largo plazo.

5. Adaptabilidad: La capacidad de adaptarse a las condiciones cambiantes del mercado es un sello distintivo de una mentalidad ganadora. Esté abierto a reevaluar sus estrategias y ajustar su cartera cuando sea necesario. Esta flexibilidad le ayudará a capitalizar nuevas oportunidades y minimizar las pérdidas potenciales.

6. Cultive una perspectiva a largo plazo: Los inversores exitosos a menudo se centran en las ganancias a largo plazo en lugar de las fluctuaciones a corto plazo. Adoptar una perspectiva a largo plazo le permite capear la volatilidad del mercado y evitar tomar decisiones apresuradas basadas en

contratiempos temporales.

7. Manténgase confiado pero humilde: La confianza es esencial para tomar decisiones de inversión, pero el exceso de confianza puede llevar a errores costosos. Desarrolle un equilibrio saludable de seguridad en sí mismo y humildad reconociendo sus limitaciones y buscando orientación de fuentes confiables cuando sea necesario.

Al cultivar una mentalidad ganadora, estará mejor equipado para navegar los desafíos del mercado de valores y tomar decisiones bien informadas que finalmente conduzcan al éxito financiero.

1.3 Evaluación de su tolerancia al riesgo

Comprender su tolerancia al riesgo es un elemento crucial para desarrollar una estrategia de inversión exitosa. La tolerancia al riesgo se refiere a la cantidad de riesgo que está dispuesto a aceptar en busca de rendimientos potenciales. Esto varía de persona a persona y está influenciado por factores como la edad, los objetivos financieros y la experiencia de inversión. Evaluar su tolerancia al riesgo le ayuda a crear una cartera de inversiones equilibrada que se alinea con su nivel de comodidad y objetivos de inversión.

Para evaluar su tolerancia al riesgo, considere los siguientes pasos:

1. Evalúe sus metas financieras: Determine sus metas financieras a corto y largo plazo, como ahorrar para una casa, financiar la educación de su hijo o prepararse para la jubilación. Conocer tus objetivos te ayudará a medir el nivel de riesgo que estás dispuesto a asumir para alcanzarlos.

2. Examine su horizonte de tiempo de inversión: Su horizonte de tiempo es el período entre su inversión inicial y cuando necesita acceder a los fondos. En general, un horizonte temporal más largo permite una mayor tolerancia al riesgo, ya que proporciona

más tiempo para recuperarse de posibles pérdidas.

3. Analice su situación financiera : Considere su situación financiera actual, incluidos sus ingresos, gastos, ahorros y deudas. Una base financiera sólida puede permitir una mayor tolerancia al riesgo, mientras que una deuda significativa o ahorros limitados pueden justificar un enfoque más conservador.

4. Reflexione sobre su experiencia de inversión: Su familiaridad con varios tipos de inversión y experiencias pasadas puede influir en su tolerancia al riesgo. Si ha navegado con éxito las fluctuaciones del mercado en el pasado, es posible que se sienta más cómodo asumiendo inversiones de mayor riesgo.

5. Evalúe su reacción emocional al riesgo: evalúe cómo maneja el estrés y la incertidumbre, ya que estas emociones a menudo acompañan a los riesgos de inversión. ¿Eres propenso a tomar decisiones impulsivas basadas en el miedo o la ansiedad? Si es así, una menor tolerancia al riesgo puede ser más adecuada para usted.

Una vez que haya evaluado su tolerancia al riesgo, puede utilizar esta información para crear una cartera diversificada adaptada a sus necesidades y preferencias específicas. Esto puede implicar asignar un cierto porcentaje de sus activos a acciones, bonos y otros vehículos de inversión en función de su tolerancia al riesgo y objetivos financieros. Al considerar cuidadosamente su tolerancia al riesgo, puede tomar decisiones de inversión más informadas y aumentar sus posibilidades de lograr el éxito financiero a largo plazo.

1.4 Elaboración de su plan de inversión personal

Crear un plan de inversión personal es esencial para establecer objetivos claros, establecer una estrategia de inversión adecuada y mantenerse en el camino hacia el éxito financiero. Su plan de inversión debe reflejar su tolerancia al riesgo, objetivos financieros y horizonte temporal. Estos son los pasos para elaborar su plan de inversión personal:

1. Defina sus metas financieras: Comience por establecer claramente sus metas financieras a corto, mediano y largo plazo. Sea específico, medible y realista, y asigne un marco de tiempo a cada objetivo. Ejemplos de metas financieras incluyen ahorrar para el pago inicial de una casa, financiar la educación universitaria de un niño o construir un nido de ahorros para la jubilación.

2. Evalúe su tolerancia al riesgo: Como se discutió en la sección 1.3, determine su tolerancia al riesgo considerando factores como su experiencia de inversión, situación financiera y respuesta emocional al riesgo. Su tolerancia al riesgo guiará sus opciones de inversión y le ayudará a crear una cartera equilibrada.

3. Determine su horizonte de tiempo de inversión: establezca un marco de tiempo para cada objetivo

financiero. Esto le ayudará a seleccionar vehículos y estrategias de inversión adecuados. En general, un horizonte temporal más largo permite una mayor asunción de riesgos, mientras que los horizontes temporales más cortos pueden requerir un enfoque más conservador.

4. Elija sus vehículos de inversión: en función de su tolerancia al riesgo y horizonte temporal, seleccione una combinación de vehículos de inversión como acciones, bonos, fondos mutuos, fondos cotizados en bolsa (ETF) y otros valores. Diversifique su cartera invirtiendo en diferentes clases de activos, sectores y regiones geográficas para reducir el riesgo y optimizar los rendimientos potenciales.

5. Asigne sus activos: Decida el porcentaje de su cartera a asignar a cada vehículo de inversión, teniendo en cuenta su tolerancia al riesgo y sus objetivos financieros. Revise y ajuste periódicamente su asignación de activos para asegurarse de que permanezca alineada con sus objetivos y condiciones del mercado.

6. Implemente su plan: Una vez que haya elaborado su plan de inversión personal, comience a invertir de acuerdo con la asignación de activos y las estrategias elegidas. Esto puede implicar abrir una cuenta de corretaje, seleccionar inversiones específicas y

establecer contribuciones regulares a sus cuentas de inversión.

7. Supervise y ajuste su plan: Revise regularmente su plan de inversión y haga un seguimiento de su progreso hacia sus metas financieras. Ajuste su plan según sea necesario para tener en cuenta los cambios en sus circunstancias personales, objetivos financieros o condiciones del mercado. Esto puede implicar reequilibrar su cartera, alterar su estrategia de inversión o modificar sus objetivos financieros.

Al elaborar un plan de inversión personal, tendrá una hoja de ruta clara para lograr sus objetivos financieros y navegar por las complejidades del mercado de valores. Este enfoque estructurado lo ayudará a mantener la disciplina, tomar decisiones informadas y, en última instancia, aumentar sus posibilidades de éxito de inversión.

Capítulo 2: Fundamentos del mercado de valores

2.1 Tipos de poblaciones y su potencial

Hay varios tipos de acciones disponibles en el mercado, cada una con su propio potencial de rendimientos y riesgos. Comprender estos tipos puede ayudarlo a construir una cartera diversa y seleccionar inversiones que se alineen con sus objetivos financieros y tolerancia al riesgo. Estos son algunos tipos comunes de acciones y su potencial:

1. Acciones ordinarias: Las acciones ordinarias representan la propiedad parcial de una empresa y dan derecho a los accionistas a una parte proporcional de las ganancias o pérdidas de la empresa. Los accionistas tienen derecho a voto en las juntas generales anuales, lo que les permite participar en las decisiones que afectan a la empresa. Las acciones comunes suelen ofrecer mayores rendimientos potenciales en comparación con otros tipos de acciones, pero también conllevan mayores riesgos.

2. Acciones preferentes: Las acciones preferentes son un híbrido entre acciones ordinarias y bonos. Pagan dividendos fijos, que tienen prioridad sobre los

dividendos de acciones ordinarias. Los accionistas preferentes generalmente no tienen derecho a voto, pero tienen un mayor derecho sobre los activos de la compañía en caso de liquidación. Las acciones preferentes generalmente ofrecen rendimientos más estables y un menor riesgo que las acciones comunes, pero su potencial de apreciación del capital es limitado.

3. Acciones de crecimiento: Las acciones de crecimiento son acciones de empresas con un alto potencial para el crecimiento futuro de los ingresos y las ganancias. Estas empresas a menudo reinvierten sus ganancias para expandir sus negocios, desarrollar nuevos productos o ingresar a nuevos mercados. Las acciones de crecimiento pueden proporcionar una apreciación significativa del capital, pero también tienden a ser más volátiles y pueden no pagar dividendos.

4. Acciones de valor: Las acciones de valor son acciones de empresas que el mercado percibe como infravaloradas, que generalmente se negocian a una relación precio-ganancias (P/E) o precio-valor contable (P/B) más baja que el promedio del mercado. Estas acciones tienen el potencial de apreciación del capital, ya que su valor de mercado finalmente refleja su verdadero valor. Las acciones de valor a menudo pagan dividendos, proporcionando a los inversores

un flujo de ingresos constante.

5. Acciones de dividendos: Las acciones de dividendos son acciones de compañías que constantemente pagan dividendos a sus accionistas. Estas acciones pueden proporcionar un flujo de ingresos regular y pueden atraer a los inversores que buscan ingresos pasivos o aquellos con una menor tolerancia al riesgo. Si bien las acciones de dividendos pueden no ofrecer una apreciación sustancial del capital, pueden proporcionar estabilidad y reducir la volatilidad general de la cartera.

6. Acciones Blue-Chip: Las acciones Blue-Chip son acciones de compañías bien establecidas, financieramente estables con un historial de desempeño consistente. Estas empresas a menudo tienen fuertes posiciones en el mercado, ventajas competitivas y la capacidad de capear las recesiones económicas. Las acciones de primera línea generalmente ofrecen riesgos más bajos y rendimientos más estables, pero pueden no tener el mismo potencial de crecimiento que otros tipos de acciones.

7. Acciones de pequeña capitalización, mediana capitalización y gran capitalización: Las acciones también se pueden clasificar en función de su capitalización de mercado, con acciones de pequeña

capitalización que representan a empresas más pequeñas, acciones de mediana capitalización que representan a empresas medianas y acciones de gran capitalización que representan a las empresas más grandes. Las acciones de pequeña capitalización suelen tener el mayor potencial de crecimiento, pero también conllevan mayores riesgos, mientras que las acciones de gran capitalización tienden a ser más estables y ofrecen menores riesgos, pero un potencial de crecimiento más modesto.

Comprender los diferentes tipos de acciones y su potencial de rendimientos y riesgos es crucial para construir una cartera diversificada que se alinee con sus objetivos de inversión y tolerancia al riesgo. Al invertir en una combinación de tipos de acciones, puede optimizar sus rendimientos potenciales al tiempo que mitiga su exposición a la volatilidad del mercado.

2.2 Lectura de estados financieros

Los estados financieros proporcionan información valiosa sobre la salud financiera y el rendimiento de una empresa. Al aprender a leer y analizar estas declaraciones, puede tomar decisiones de inversión más informadas y evaluar mejor el potencial de una empresa. Hay tres estados financieros principales a considerar:

1. Balance: El balance general proporciona una instantánea de la posición financiera de una empresa en un momento específico. Se divide en activos, pasivos y patrimonio de los accionistas. La ecuación del balance es: Activos = Pasivos + Patrimonio de los accionistas.

- Activos: Recursos propiedad de la empresa, incluyendo efectivo, inventario, propiedad y equipo.
- Pasivos: Obligaciones financieras que la empresa debe a otros, como préstamos, cuentas por pagar y deuda a largo plazo.
- Patrimonio del Accionariado: El interés residual en los activos de la empresa después de deducir los pasivos, también conocidos como activos netos o patrimonio neto.

2. Estado de resultados: El estado de resultados

(también conocido como el estado de pérdidas y ganancias) muestra el desempeño financiero de una empresa durante un período específico, generalmente un trimestre o un año. Muestra ingresos, gastos e ingresos netos.

- Ingresos: Dinero ganado por la empresa de sus actividades comerciales, como ventas o tarifas de servicio.
- Gastos: Costos incurridos por la empresa para generar ingresos, incluido el costo de los bienes vendidos, los gastos operativos y los impuestos.
- Utilidad Neta: La diferencia entre ingresos y gastos, que representa la ganancia o pérdida de la compañía durante el período del informe.

3. Estado de flujo de efectivo: El estado de flujo de efectivo muestra el movimiento de efectivo dentro y fuera de una empresa durante un período específico. Se divide en tres secciones: actividades operativas, actividades de inversión y actividades de financiación.

Actividades operativas: efectivo generado por las operaciones comerciales principales de una empresa, como tarifas de ventas o servicios, menos efectivo utilizado para gastos operativos.
- Actividades de inversión: efectivo utilizado para

invertir en el crecimiento de la empresa, como la compra de propiedades o equipos, o efectivo recibido de la venta de activos.

- Actividades de financiamiento: efectivo recibido o pagado a los inversores, como la emisión o recompra de acciones, el pago de dividendos o el endeudamiento y el pago de deudas.

Al analizar los estados financieros, los inversores a menudo buscan tendencias, proporciones y comparaciones con otras compañías en la misma industria. Algunas métricas clave a considerar incluyen:

- Ganancias por acción (EPS): Ingresos netos divididos por el número de acciones en circulación, indicando la porción de la ganancia de una empresa asignada a cada acción.

- Relación precio-ganancias (P/E): Precio de mercado por acción dividido por EPS, que muestra la valoración de una acción en relación con sus ganancias.

- Relación precio-valor contable (P/B): Precio de mercado por acción dividido por el valor contable por acción (patrimonio neto dividido por el número de acciones en circulación), que mide la valoración de una acción en relación con su valor liquidativo.

- Dividend Yield: Dividendo anual por acción dividido

por el precio de mercado por acción, mostrando los ingresos generados por una acción en relación con su precio.

Al aprender a leer e interpretar los estados financieros, puede obtener una comprensión más profunda de la salud financiera de una empresa y tomar decisiones de inversión más informadas. Este conocimiento puede ayudarlo a identificar posibles oportunidades de inversión y evaluar los riesgos asociados con acciones individuales.

2.3 Análisis de tendencias e indicadores del mercado

Analizar las tendencias e indicadores del mercado es esencial para comprender la dirección general del mercado de valores y tomar decisiones de inversión informadas. Los inversores utilizan diversos métodos y herramientas para identificar tendencias, detectar oportunidades potenciales y medir el sentimiento del mercado. Aquí hay algunas tendencias e indicadores clave del mercado a considerar:

1. Índices de mercado: Los índices de mercado proporcionan una instantánea del rendimiento general de un mercado o segmento específico. Los índices populares incluyen el S&P 500, el Dow Jones Industrial Average (DJIA) y el NASDAQ Composite. Al rastrear estos índices, los inversores pueden medir la dirección general del mercado e identificar tendencias en sectores o industrias específicas.

2. Medias móviles: Las medias móviles ayudan a suavizar las fluctuaciones de precios y revelan tendencias subyacentes en el precio de una acción. Los inversores a menudo utilizan medias móviles simples (SMA) o medias móviles exponenciales (EMA) durante diferentes períodos de tiempo (por ejemplo, 50 días, 100 días o 200 días) para identificar

los niveles de soporte y resistencia y las posibles reversiones de tendencia.

3. Indicadores técnicos: Los indicadores técnicos son cálculos matemáticos basados en el precio, el volumen u otros datos de mercado de una acción. Pueden ayudar a identificar patrones, tendencias y posibles señales de compra o venta. Los indicadores técnicos comunes incluyen el Índice de Fuerza Relativa (RSI), la Divergencia de Convergencia de la Media Móvil (MACD) y las Bandas de Bollinger.

4. Volumen: El volumen se refiere al número de acciones negociadas durante un período específico. Un volumen de negociación alto puede indicar un fuerte interés en una acción, mientras que un volumen bajo puede sugerir un interés limitado. El análisis del volumen puede ayudar a los inversores a confirmar tendencias e identificar posibles rupturas o reversiones.

5. Sentimiento del mercado: El sentimiento del mercado se refiere a la actitud general de los inversores hacia un mercado o acción en particular. El sentimiento positivo puede impulsar los precios al alza, mientras que el sentimiento negativo puede conducir a una disminución de los precios. Los inversores a menudo utilizan indicadores de sentimiento, como la relación Put/Call, el índice de

volatilidad (VIX) o el índice de porcentaje alcista (BPI), para medir el sentimiento del mercado y predecir los movimientos futuros de los precios.

6. Indicadores económicos: Los indicadores económicos proporcionan información sobre la salud de la economía y pueden influir en las tendencias del mercado de valores. Los indicadores económicos clave incluyen el crecimiento del PIB, las tasas de desempleo, los datos de inflación y las tasas de interés. Los inversores deben monitorear estos indicadores para medir el entorno económico general y evaluar el impacto potencial en acciones o sectores individuales.

7. Informes de ganancias: Las empresas publican informes trimestrales de ganancias, que pueden influir significativamente en los precios de las acciones y las tendencias del mercado. Las fuertes ganancias pueden impulsar los precios de las acciones, mientras que los resultados decepcionantes pueden conducir a caídas de precios. Los inversores deben realizar un seguimiento de las publicaciones de ganancias y analizar los resultados para determinar el impacto potencial en sus inversiones.

Al analizar las tendencias e indicadores del mercado, los inversores pueden obtener información valiosa sobre la dirección del mercado de valores e identificar posibles oportunidades de inversión. Este conocimiento puede ayudar a los inversores a tomar decisiones más informadas, gestionar el riesgo y, en última instancia, lograr un mayor éxito en el mercado de valores.

2.4 El papel de la economía global

La economía global juega un papel crítico para influir en el desempeño del mercado de valores y las inversiones individuales. Comprender la interconexión de las economías y el impacto de los eventos globales puede ayudar a los inversores a tomar decisiones más informadas y gestionar mejor el riesgo. Aquí hay algunos aspectos clave de la economía global que pueden influir en el mercado de valores:

1. Relaciones comerciales: El comercio internacional es vital para el crecimiento económico, ya que los países intercambian bienes y servicios para satisfacer las demandas internas y expandir sus mercados. Los acuerdos comerciales, los aranceles y las barreras comerciales pueden afectar el flujo de bienes y servicios e impactar la rentabilidad de las empresas involucradas en el comercio internacional. Los inversores deben monitorear las relaciones comerciales entre los países y considerar las posibles implicaciones para sus inversiones.

2. Tipos de cambio: El valor de una moneda en relación con otra, conocido como el tipo de cambio, puede tener un impacto significativo en el mercado de valores. Las fluctuaciones en los tipos de cambio pueden afectar la competitividad de las

exportaciones, el costo de las importaciones y el valor de las inversiones extranjeras. Los inversores deben considerar el impacto potencial de los movimientos de divisas en sus carteras de inversión y pueden utilizar estrategias como la cobertura de divisas para mitigar el riesgo cambiario.

3. Tasas de interés: Los bancos centrales, como la Reserva Federal, el Banco Central Europeo y el Banco de Japón, establecen tasas de interés para administrar la inflación, el crecimiento económico y la estabilidad financiera. Los cambios en las tasas de interés pueden influir en los costos de endeudamiento, el gasto del consumidor y las ganancias corporativas, afectando así los precios de las acciones. Los inversores deben prestar mucha atención a las políticas del banco central y las decisiones sobre los tipos de interés a la hora de evaluar las oportunidades de inversión.

4. Eventos geopolíticos: Los eventos geopolíticos, como guerras, disturbios políticos y disputas diplomáticas, pueden crear incertidumbre en la economía global e impactar el mercado de valores. Tales eventos pueden afectar la confianza de los inversores, interrumpir el comercio y conducir a cambios en las políticas gubernamentales que influyen en el crecimiento económico y la rentabilidad corporativa. Los inversores deben

monitorear los eventos geopolíticos y evaluar su impacto potencial en el mercado de valores y las inversiones individuales.

5. Crecimiento económico global: El crecimiento general de la economía global, medido por indicadores como el Producto Interno Bruto (PIB), puede influir en el mercado de valores. El fuerte crecimiento económico mundial generalmente respalda mayores ganancias corporativas y precios de acciones, mientras que las desaceleraciones económicas o recesiones pueden conducir a menores ganancias y caídas del mercado de valores. Los inversores deben seguir las tendencias de crecimiento económico mundial y considerar las posibles implicaciones para sus inversiones.

6. Mercados emergentes: Los mercados emergentes, como China, India y Brasil, ofrecen un potencial de crecimiento significativo, pero también conllevan mayores riesgos debido a la inestabilidad política, las fluctuaciones monetarias y la volatilidad económica. Invertir en mercados emergentes puede proporcionar beneficios de diversificación y mejorar los rendimientos de la cartera, pero requiere un análisis cuidadoso y una gestión de riesgos. Los inversores deben considerar las oportunidades y los riesgos asociados con los mercados emergentes al construir sus carteras de inversión.

Comprender el papel de la economía global en el mercado de valores puede ayudar a los inversores a navegar por las complejidades de la inversión internacional y tomar decisiones más informadas. Al considerar el impacto de los factores económicos globales en las inversiones individuales y en el mercado en general, los inversores pueden gestionar mejor el riesgo, aprovechar las oportunidades y, en última instancia, lograr un mayor éxito en el mercado de valores.

Capítulo 3: El arte de la selección de acciones

3.1 Análisis fundamental para el éxito a largo plazo

El análisis fundamental es un método para evaluar las acciones mediante la evaluación de la salud financiera subyacente y el rendimiento de una empresa. Al centrarse en los fundamentos de una empresa, los inversores pueden identificar acciones infravaloradas con un fuerte potencial de crecimiento y tomar decisiones más informadas para el éxito a largo plazo. Aquí hay algunos aspectos clave del análisis fundamental a considerar:

1. Estados financieros: Como se mencionó anteriormente, los estados financieros proporcionan información valiosa sobre la salud financiera y el desempeño de una empresa. Analizar el balance general, el estado de resultados y el estado de flujo de efectivo de una empresa puede ayudar a los inversores a comprender su rentabilidad, solvencia y perspectivas de crecimiento.

2. Ratios financieros: Los ratios financieros son herramientas útiles para comparar el rendimiento de una empresa con sus pares o puntos de referencia de la industria. Algunos ratios importantes a considerar

incluyen la relación precio-ganancias (P/E), la relación precio-valor contable (P/B), la rentabilidad por dividendo, el retorno sobre el capital (ROE) y la relación deuda-capital. Estos ratios pueden ayudar a los inversores a identificar acciones infravaloradas, evaluar las perspectivas de crecimiento de una empresa y evaluar su estabilidad financiera.

3. Análisis de la industria: Comprender la industria en la que opera una empresa es crucial para evaluar su posición competitiva y potencial de crecimiento. Los inversores deben investigar las tendencias de la industria, el tamaño del mercado, los competidores clave y las barreras de entrada para obtener información sobre la posición de mercado de la empresa y el potencial de crecimiento futuro.

4. Equipo directivo: La calidad del equipo directivo de una empresa puede influir significativamente en su éxito. Los inversores deben evaluar la experiencia, el historial y el desempeño del liderazgo de la empresa para medir su capacidad para impulsar el crecimiento y navegar por los desafíos.

5. Ventaja competitiva: Una empresa con una fuerte ventaja competitiva está mejor posicionada para generar un crecimiento constante y ganancias a largo plazo. Los inversores deben identificar a las empresas con productos, servicios o modelos de negocio únicos

que los diferencien de los competidores y creen barreras de entrada para los nuevos participantes en el mercado.

6. Perspectivas de crecimiento: Evaluar las perspectivas de crecimiento de una empresa es fundamental para determinar su potencial de éxito a largo plazo. Los inversores deben considerar factores como el crecimiento de los ingresos y las ganancias, la cuota de mercado, los planes de expansión y la cartera de productos para medir el potencial de crecimiento futuro de una empresa.

7. Valoración: Determinar si una acción está infravalorada o sobrevalorada es una parte esencial del análisis fundamental. Los inversores pueden utilizar métodos de valoración como el análisis de flujo de caja descontado (DCF), la valoración relativa (comparando los índices financieros con sus pares) o los modelos de descuento de dividendos (DDM) para estimar el valor intrínseco de una acción e identificar posibles oportunidades de inversión.

Al realizar un análisis fundamental exhaustivo, los inversores pueden obtener una comprensión más profunda de la salud financiera, la posición competitiva y el potencial de crecimiento de una empresa. Este conocimiento puede ayudarles a identificar acciones infravaloradas con fuertes perspectivas a largo plazo y tomar decisiones más informadas para lograr el éxito en el mercado de valores.

3.2 Análisis técnico para la sincronización de precisión

El análisis técnico es un método para evaluar las acciones mediante el análisis de datos históricos de precios y volúmenes para identificar patrones y tendencias que pueden ayudar a predecir futuros movimientos de precios. Mediante el uso del análisis técnico, los inversores pueden cronometrar sus puntos de entrada y salida con mayor precisión, maximizando sus rendimientos potenciales. Aquí hay algunos aspectos clave del análisis técnico a considerar:

1. Patrones de gráficos: Los patrones de gráficos son representaciones visuales de los movimientos de precios a lo largo del tiempo que pueden ayudar a identificar tendencias, reversiones o señales de continuación. Algunos patrones de gráficos comunes incluyen cabeza y hombros, dobles tops e inferiores, triángulos y banderas. Al reconocer estos patrones, los inversores pueden tomar decisiones más informadas sobre cuándo comprar o vender una acción.

2. Líneas de tendencia: Las líneas de tendencia son líneas dibujadas en un gráfico de precios para conectar una serie de máximos o mínimos, que representan los niveles de soporte y resistencia.

Pueden ayudar a los inversores a identificar la dirección de la tendencia del mercado (hacia arriba, hacia abajo o hacia los lados) y determinar los posibles puntos de entrada y salida.

3. Medias móviles: Como se mencionó anteriormente, las medias móviles se utilizan para suavizar las fluctuaciones de precios y revelar las tendencias subyacentes. Los inversores a menudo utilizan las medias móviles como una herramienta simple para identificar posibles niveles de soporte o resistencia, reversiones de tendencia y puntos de entrada o salida.

4. Indicadores técnicos: Los indicadores técnicos son cálculos matemáticos basados en el precio, el volumen u otros datos de mercado que pueden proporcionar información sobre las tendencias del mercado y las posibles señales de compra o venta. Algunos indicadores técnicos populares incluyen el Índice de Fuerza Relativa (RSI), la Divergencia de Convergencia de la Media Móvil (MACD), las Bandas de Bollinger y el Oscilador Estocástico. Estos indicadores pueden ayudar a los inversores a cronometrar sus operaciones de manera más efectiva y gestionar el riesgo.

5. Análisis de volumen: Analizar el volumen de negociación puede ayudar a los inversores a medir

la fuerza de los movimientos de precios e identificar posibles rupturas o reversiones. Un volumen de negociación alto puede indicar un fuerte interés en una acción, mientras que un volumen bajo puede indicar un interés limitado. Al monitorear los cambios de volumen, los inversores pueden obtener información valiosa sobre el sentimiento del mercado y las posibles tendencias de precios.

6. Soporte y resistencia: Los niveles de soporte y resistencia son puntos de precio en los que el precio de una acción históricamente ha tenido dificultades para moverse por encima (resistencia) o por debajo (soporte). La identificación de estos niveles puede ayudar a los inversores a determinar los posibles puntos de entrada y salida, así como a evaluar la probabilidad de rupturas o reversiones de precios.

7. Marcos temporales: El análisis técnico se puede aplicar a diferentes marcos de tiempo, como gráficos intradiarios, diarios, semanales o mensuales. La elección del marco de tiempo adecuado depende del estilo de negociación y el horizonte de inversión del inversor. Los operadores a corto plazo pueden centrarse en gráficos intradía o diarios, mientras que los inversores a largo plazo pueden preferir gráficos semanales o mensuales.

Al dominar el arte del análisis técnico, los inversores

pueden mejorar su tiempo y precisión en el mercado de valores, maximizando sus rendimientos potenciales. La combinación del análisis técnico con el análisis fundamental puede proporcionar una comprensión más completa del potencial de una acción, ayudando a los inversores a tomar decisiones más informadas y lograr un mayor éxito en el mercado de valores.

3.3 Valor vs. inversión de crecimiento

La inversión en valor y crecimiento son dos enfoques distintos para la selección de acciones, cada uno con su propio conjunto de criterios y recompensas potenciales. Comprender las diferencias entre estos estilos puede ayudar a los inversores a desarrollar una estrategia que se adapte a sus objetivos de inversión y tolerancia al riesgo. Aquí hay una comparación de la inversión en valor y crecimiento:

Inversión en valor:

Los inversores de valor buscan identificar acciones infravaloradas con fundamentos sólidos que tienen el potencial de apreciarse con el tiempo. Estos inversores creen que el mercado ocasionalmente valora mal las acciones, creando oportunidades para comprar compañías de alta calidad con un descuento. Los aspectos clave de la inversión en valor incluyen:

1. Concéntrese en los fundamentos: los inversores de valor priorizan la salud financiera y el rendimiento de una empresa, analizando estados financieros, ratios y otras métricas para determinar el valor intrínseco de una acción.

2. Margen de seguridad: Al comprar acciones con un

descuento sobre su valor intrínseco, los inversores de valor tienen como objetivo crear un margen de seguridad que los proteja de posibles pérdidas y aumente el potencial de apreciación del capital.

3. Perspectiva a largo plazo: La inversión de valor generalmente implica un horizonte de inversión a largo plazo, ya que las acciones infravaloradas pueden tardar en desarrollar todo su potencial.

4. Dividendos e ingresos: Los inversores de valor a menudo favorecen las acciones con rendimientos de dividendos atractivos, ya que proporcionan un flujo constante de ingresos y pueden contribuir a los rendimientos totales.

Inversión de crecimiento:

Los inversores de crecimiento se centran en empresas con un potencial de crecimiento superior a la media, buscando acciones que se espera que generen un fuerte crecimiento de los ingresos y las ganancias a lo largo del tiempo. Estos inversores están dispuestos a pagar una prima por acciones con altas perspectivas de crecimiento, creyendo que el potencial de apreciación del capital supera los riesgos. Los aspectos clave de la inversión de crecimiento incluyen:

1. Énfasis en las métricas de crecimiento: los inversores de crecimiento priorizan métricas como el crecimiento de los ingresos, el crecimiento de las ganancias y la expansión de la cuota de mercado al evaluar las acciones.

2. Altas expectativas: Las acciones de crecimiento suelen tener altos ratios precio-beneficio (P/E) y otras métricas de valoración, lo que refleja las altas expectativas del mercado para el crecimiento futuro.

3. Enfoque a corto plazo: La inversión de crecimiento puede implicar un horizonte de inversión más corto que la inversión de valor, ya que las acciones de crecimiento pueden ser más sensibles a las fluctuaciones y el sentimiento del mercado.

4. Apreciación del capital: Los inversores en crecimiento buscan principalmente la apreciación del capital en lugar de dividendos, ya que las empresas en crecimiento a menudo reinvierten las ganancias para impulsar una mayor expansión.

Ni la inversión de valor ni la de crecimiento son inherentemente superiores, y el mejor enfoque a menudo depende de los objetivos individuales de un inversor, la tolerancia al riesgo y el horizonte de inversión. Algunos inversores pueden optar por combinar elementos de ambos estilos para crear una cartera equilibrada que ofrezca tanto apreciación de capital como potencial de ingresos. Al comprender las diferencias entre la inversión de valor y la inversión de crecimiento, los inversores pueden tomar decisiones más informadas y desarrollar una estrategia que se alinee con sus objetivos y preferencias únicos.

3.4 Acciones de dividendos: un flujo de ingresos constante

Las acciones de dividendos representan una opción de inversión atractiva para aquellos que buscan un flujo constante de ingresos junto con una posible apreciación del capital. Las empresas que pagan dividendos distribuyen una parte de sus ganancias a los accionistas, generalmente trimestralmente. Invertir en acciones que pagan dividendos puede proporcionar varios beneficios, que incluyen:

1. Ingresos regulares: Los dividendos proporcionan una fuente predecible de ingresos para los inversores, que puede ser particularmente atractiva para los jubilados o aquellos que buscan complementar sus ingresos actuales.

2. Rendimientos compuestos: Reinvertir dividendos a través de un plan de reinversión de dividendos (DRIP) puede mejorar significativamente los rendimientos a largo plazo al permitir a los inversores comprar acciones adicionales sin incurrir en costos de transacción. Con el tiempo, esto puede conducir a un crecimiento exponencial tanto en el número de acciones poseídas como en el valor total de la inversión.

3. Volatilidad reducida: Las acciones que pagan

dividendos tienden a ser menos volátiles que las acciones que no pagan dividendos, ya que el flujo de ingresos regular puede ayudar a amortiguar el impacto de las fluctuaciones del mercado. Esto puede ser especialmente beneficioso para los inversores con aversión al riesgo o aquellos con un horizonte de inversión más corto.

4. Ventajas fiscales: Dependiendo de la situación fiscal y la jurisdicción de un inversor, los ingresos por dividendos pueden gravarse a una tasa más baja que otras formas de ingresos de inversión, como intereses o ganancias de capital.

5. Indicador de calidad: Las empresas con un historial de pago de dividendos consistentes a menudo están bien establecidas y son financieramente estables, lo que sugiere fundamentos sólidos y un menor riesgo en comparación con las acciones que no pagan dividendos.

Al evaluar las acciones de dividendos, los inversores deben considerar los siguientes factores:

1. Rendimiento de dividendos: El rendimiento de dividendos se calcula dividiendo el dividendo anual por acción por el precio actual de la acción. Un rendimiento más alto puede indicar un flujo de ingresos más atractivo, pero también puede indicar

un mayor riesgo o problemas potenciales con los fundamentos de la empresa.

2. Relación de pago de dividendos: La relación de pago de dividendos se calcula dividiendo los dividendos totales pagados por los ingresos netos de la compañía. Un índice de pago más bajo sugiere que la compañía está reteniendo más ganancias para la reinversión y el crecimiento, mientras que un índice más alto puede indicar un potencial de crecimiento limitado o tensión financiera.

3. Tasa de crecimiento de dividendos: La tasa de crecimiento de dividendos mide cuánto ha aumentado el dividendo de una empresa con el tiempo. Una tasa de crecimiento de dividendos consistente puede indicar el compromiso de una empresa de devolver valor a los accionistas y su capacidad para generar ganancias crecientes.

4. Aristócratas de dividendos: Los aristócratas de dividendos son compañías que han aumentado constantemente sus pagos de dividendos durante al menos 25 años consecutivos. Estas acciones pueden ofrecer una combinación de estabilidad, ingresos y apreciación potencial del capital.

5. Seguridad de dividendos: Evaluar la seguridad de un dividendo es esencial para garantizar que la

empresa pueda mantener o aumentar sus pagos de dividendos. Los inversores deben considerar factores como la estabilidad de las ganancias, los niveles de deuda y el flujo de efectivo al evaluar la seguridad de los dividendos.

Al seleccionar cuidadosamente las acciones de dividendos, los inversores pueden crear un flujo de ingresos confiable y potencialmente beneficiarse de la apreciación del capital a lo largo del tiempo. Equilibrar una cartera con acciones de dividendos y otras estrategias de inversión puede ayudar a los inversores a alcanzar sus objetivos financieros y gestionar el riesgo de manera efectiva.

Capítulo 4: Técnicas avanzadas de trading

4.1 Negociación de opciones para apalancamiento y flexibilidad

El comercio de opciones es una estrategia de inversión avanzada que permite a los inversores obtener exposición a una acción u otro activo sin poseerlo realmente. Los contratos de opciones otorgan al comprador el derecho, pero no la obligación, de comprar o vender un activo subyacente a un precio específico (el "precio de ejercicio") antes de una fecha de vencimiento predeterminada. Hay dos tipos de contratos de opciones: calls (el derecho a comprar) y puts (el derecho a vender). El comercio de opciones puede proporcionar varios beneficios, incluyendo apalancamiento, flexibilidad y gestión de riesgos. Aquí hay algunos aspectos clave del comercio de opciones:

1. Apalancamiento: Los contratos de opciones permiten a los inversores controlar una gran cantidad de un activo subyacente con una inversión relativamente pequeña. Este apalancamiento puede magnificar las ganancias potenciales, pero también aumenta el riesgo, por lo que es crucial para los inversores gestionar sus posiciones y exposición con

cuidado.

2. Flexibilidad: El comercio de opciones ofrece flexibilidad en términos de estrategias y resultados potenciales. Los inversores pueden usar opciones para especular, cubrir o generar ingresos. Por ejemplo, un inversor puede usar opciones de compra para beneficiarse de un posible aumento en el precio de una acción, opciones de venta para protegerse contra una posible disminución o vender opciones para generar ingresos de las primas cobradas.

3. Gestión de riesgos: Las opciones se pueden utilizar como una herramienta de gestión de riesgos al proporcionar una pérdida máxima predefinida para el comprador. Lo máximo que un comprador de opciones puede perder es la prima pagada por el contrato, mientras que las ganancias potenciales pueden ser ilimitadas para las opciones de compra y sustanciales para las opciones de venta. Este riesgo predefinido hace que las opciones sean una estrategia atractiva para los inversores que buscan limitar sus pérdidas potenciales.

4. Decaimiento del tiempo: Los contratos de opciones tienen una fecha de vencimiento, después de la cual pierden su valor. A medida que se acerca la fecha de vencimiento, el valor de tiempo de la opción disminuye, un fenómeno conocido como

"decaimiento del tiempo". Esta decadencia puede funcionar en contra de los compradores y a favor de los vendedores, por lo que es importante que los inversores consideren el horizonte temporal de sus estrategias de opciones.

5. Precio de la prima: El precio de una opción, conocido como "prima", está influenciado por factores como el precio del activo subyacente, el precio de ejercicio, el tiempo hasta el vencimiento, la volatilidad y las tasas de interés. Comprender estos factores puede ayudar a los inversores a determinar el valor razonable de una opción e identificar posibles oportunidades comerciales.

6. Estrategias comerciales: Existen numerosas estrategias de negociación de opciones, que van desde simples hasta complejas, que pueden ayudar a los inversores a alcanzar sus objetivos de inversión. Algunas estrategias populares incluyen llamadas cubiertas, puts protectores, extensiones verticales, cóndores de hierro y horcajadas.

7. Comprender los riesgos: Si bien el comercio de opciones puede ofrecer beneficios significativos, también implica riesgos, como pérdidas relacionadas con el apalancamiento, deterioro del tiempo y posible falta de liquidez. Es esencial que los inversores se eduquen sobre los riesgos y la mecánica del comercio

de opciones antes de participar en estas estrategias avanzadas.

El comercio de opciones puede proporcionar a los inversores oportunidades de apalancamiento, flexibilidad y gestión de riesgos que el comercio tradicional de acciones puede no ofrecer. Al comprender los conceptos básicos del comercio de opciones y administrar cuidadosamente sus posiciones y riesgos, los inversores pueden mejorar potencialmente sus rendimientos y alcanzar sus objetivos financieros.

4.2 Venta en corto con fines de lucro en mercados bajistas

La venta en corto es una estrategia comercial avanzada que permite a los inversores beneficiarse de la disminución de los precios de las acciones. Implica tomar prestadas acciones de una acción de un corredor, venderlas en el mercado abierto y luego recomprar las acciones más tarde a un precio más bajo para devolverlas al prestamista. Mediante la venta en corto, los inversores pueden capitalizar los mercados bajistas o las tendencias a la baja en acciones individuales. Estos son algunos aspectos clave de la venta en corto:

1. Potencial de ganancias: La venta en corto permite a los inversores beneficiarse de la caída de los precios de las acciones, brindando la oportunidad de generar rendimientos en mercados bajistas o durante las correcciones del mercado.

2. Gestión de riesgos: La venta en corto puede servir como una herramienta de gestión de riesgos al permitir a los inversores cubrir sus posiciones largas. Si un inversor mantiene una posición larga en una acción o cartera y anticipa una posible disminución, puede vender en corto la misma acción o un activo correlacionado para compensar posibles pérdidas.

3. Eficiencia del mercado: La venta en corto puede contribuir a la eficiencia del mercado al proporcionar liquidez y ayudar a corregir las acciones sobrevaloradas. Cuando los vendedores en corto identifican acciones sobrevaloradas y las venden, ejercen una presión a la baja sobre el precio de la acción, acercándola a su valor razonable.

4. Requisitos de margen: La venta en corto generalmente requiere una cuenta de margen, ya que el inversionista debe pedir prestadas acciones para vender en corto. El inversionista debe mantener un cierto nivel de equidad en la cuenta, conocido como el requisito de margen, que puede variar según el corredor y las acciones que se están acortando.

5. Riesgos y limitaciones: La venta en corto conlleva varios riesgos y limitaciones, incluidas pérdidas potencialmente ilimitadas, apretones cortos y restricciones en la venta en corto de ciertas acciones. La pérdida potencial en una posición corta es teóricamente ilimitada, ya que el precio de una acción puede continuar aumentando indefinidamente. Las apretones cortas ocurren cuando los vendedores en corto se ven obligados a recomprar acciones para cubrir sus posiciones, lo que eleva aún más el precio de las acciones. Además, las restricciones regulatorias pueden limitar la

capacidad de vender en corto ciertas acciones o requerir que los vendedores en corto cumplan con reglas específicas.

6. Tiempo y análisis: La venta en corto exitosa requiere un momento preciso y un análisis de las tendencias del mercado, los fundamentos de las acciones y el sentimiento de los inversores. Es esencial que los vendedores en corto supervisen de cerca sus posiciones y tengan una estrategia de salida clara para gestionar el riesgo.

7. Interés corto y días a cubrir: El interés corto, el número de acciones vendidas a corto plazo y los días a cubrir, la relación entre el interés corto y el volumen diario promedio de negociación de la acción, pueden proporcionar información valiosa sobre el sentimiento del mercado y el potencial de una contracción corta. Un alto interés corto y una alta proporción de días a cobertura pueden indicar una mayor probabilidad de una contracción corta.

La venta en corto puede proporcionar a los inversores la oportunidad de obtener ganancias en los mercados bajistas y gestionar el riesgo en sus carteras. Sin embargo, también implica riesgos significativos y requiere una comprensión profunda de la dinámica del mercado y el análisis de acciones. Al administrar cuidadosamente sus posiciones cortas y mantenerse informados sobre las tendencias y los riesgos del mercado, los inversores pueden utilizar las ventas en corto como una herramienta valiosa en su estrategia de inversión general.

4.3 Comercio de margen: la espada de doble filo

El comercio de margen es una estrategia de inversión avanzada que implica pedir dinero prestado a un corredor para comprar más acciones de una acción u otro activo financiero de lo que el inversor podría permitirse. Mediante el uso del apalancamiento, el comercio de margen puede amplificar las ganancias potenciales, pero también aumenta los riesgos asociados con la inversión. Aquí hay algunos aspectos clave del comercio de margen:

1. Apalancamiento: El comercio de margen permite a los inversores apalancar su capital, lo que podría aumentar los rendimientos de las operaciones exitosas. Sin embargo, este apalancamiento también amplifica las pérdidas en operaciones fallidas, por lo que es esencial que los inversores gestionen el riesgo con cuidado.

2. Cuenta de margen: Para participar en el comercio de margen, los inversores deben abrir una cuenta de margen con su corredor. Esta cuenta les permite pedir fondos prestados, y los valores comprados sirven como garantía para el préstamo. El préstamo de margen viene con intereses, que el inversor debe pagar independientemente del rendimiento de la inversión.

3. Requisitos de margen: Los corredores tienen requisitos de margen específicos, que dictan la cantidad mínima de capital que un inversionista debe mantener en su cuenta de margen. Si el capital en la cuenta cae por debajo de este nivel, el inversor se enfrentará a una llamada de margen, lo que les exigirá depositar fondos adicionales o vender activos para cumplir con el requisito.

4. Margen de mantenimiento: El margen de mantenimiento es el porcentaje mínimo de capital que un inversor debe mantener en su cuenta de margen en relación con el valor total de los activos. Si el capital de un inversor cae por debajo del margen de mantenimiento, recibirá una llamada de margen y debe tomar medidas para cumplir con el requisito.

5. Riesgo de liquidación: En el caso de una llamada de margen, si un inversor no puede depositar fondos adicionales o vender activos para cumplir con los requisitos de margen, el corredor puede liquidar algunas o todas las posiciones del inversor para cubrir el déficit. Esta liquidación forzosa puede resultar en pérdidas significativas y puede ocurrir a precios de mercado desfavorables.

6. Costos de interés: El comercio de margen implica pedir dinero prestado, que viene con costos

de intereses. Estos cargos por intereses pueden acumularse con el tiempo y erosionar las ganancias potenciales, particularmente en los casos en que las inversiones no funcionan como se espera o cuando las tasas de interés son altas.

7. Gestión de riesgos: Debido al aumento de los riesgos asociados con el comercio de margen, es crucial que los inversores implementen estrategias de gestión de riesgos. Estos pueden incluir el uso de órdenes de stop-loss, el mantenimiento de una cartera diversa y el monitoreo de las posiciones de cerca para evitar llamadas de margen y liquidaciones forzadas.

El comercio de margen puede ser una herramienta poderosa para los inversores que buscan mejorar sus rendimientos, pero también conlleva riesgos significativos. Es esencial que los inversores comprendan la mecánica del comercio de margen y administren cuidadosamente sus posiciones, niveles de capital y riesgos para aprovechar al máximo esta espada de doble filo.

4.4 El poder de los ETF apalancados

Los fondos cotizados en bolsa (ETF) apalancados son productos de inversión especializados que tienen como objetivo amplificar los rendimientos diarios de un índice o punto de referencia subyacente, generalmente mediante el uso de derivados financieros e instrumentos de deuda. Estos ETF pueden proporcionar a los inversores ganancias significativas en un período corto, pero también conllevan mayores riesgos en comparación con los ETF tradicionales. Estos son algunos aspectos clave de los ETF apalancados:

1. Ratios de apalancamiento: Los ETF apalancados ofrecen diferentes niveles de apalancamiento, que generalmente oscilan entre 2x y 3x el rendimiento diario del índice subyacente. Esto significa que si el índice aumenta un 1% en un día determinado, un ETF apalancado 2x apuntaría a lograr un rendimiento del 2%, mientras que un ETF apalancado 3x apuntaría a un rendimiento del 3%. Por el contrario, si el índice disminuye un 1%, los ETF apalancados perderían un 2% y un 3%, respectivamente.

2. Reinicios diarios: Los ETF apalancados están diseñados para proporcionar su apalancamiento objetivo a diario, lo que significa que restablecen

su exposición al final de cada día de negociación. Este restablecimiento diario puede provocar efectos compuestos a lo largo del tiempo, lo que hace que el rendimiento del ETF se desvíe del múltiplo esperado del rendimiento del índice durante períodos más largos.

3. Efectos compuestos: Debido a su función de reinicio diario, los ETF apalancados pueden experimentar efectos compuestos significativos, tanto positivos como negativos. En los mercados de tendencia, estos efectos compuestos pueden funcionar a favor del inversor, mejorando los rendimientos. Sin embargo, en mercados volátiles o de rango limitado, los efectos compuestos pueden resultar en pérdidas significativas o bajo rendimiento en comparación con el múltiplo esperado del rendimiento del índice.

4. Gestión de riesgos: Invertir en ETFs apalancados implica un mayor riesgo que los ETFs tradicionales, por lo que es esencial que los inversores implementen estrategias de gestión de riesgos. Estos pueden incluir el establecimiento de órdenes de stop-loss, la diversificación de las inversiones y el seguimiento de las posiciones de cerca para evitar pérdidas excesivas.

5. ETF apalancados cortos e inversos: Además de los ETF apalancados tradicionales, también hay

ETF apalancados inversos que tienen como objetivo proporcionar el rendimiento opuesto del índice subyacente. Estos ETF se pueden utilizar para beneficiarse de los mercados en declive o cubrir posiciones largas en una cartera.

6. Índices de gastos: Los ETF apalancados tienden a tener índices de gastos más altos que los ETF tradicionales debido a la complejidad de sus estrategias y los costos asociados con el uso de derivados y préstamos. Estos gastos más altos pueden afectar los rendimientos potenciales de los ETF.

7. Estrategias comerciales: Los ETF apalancados suelen ser los más adecuados para estrategias comerciales a corto plazo y jugadas tácticas en lugar de inversiones a largo plazo. Debido a su función de reinicio diario y al potencial de efectos compuestos significativos, mantener ETF apalancados durante períodos prolongados puede conducir a resultados inesperados y bajo rendimiento.

Los ETF apalancados pueden brindar a los inversores la oportunidad de lograr rendimientos descomunales en un corto período de tiempo, pero también conllevan mayores riesgos y potencial de pérdidas significativas. Es crucial que los inversores comprendan la mecánica de los ETF apalancados y gestionen cuidadosamente sus posiciones, riesgos y expectativas al incorporar estas poderosas herramientas en sus estrategias de inversión.

Capítulo 5: Creación de una cartera diversificada

5.1 La importancia de la asignación de activos

La asignación de activos es el proceso de dividir una cartera de inversiones entre varias clases de activos, como acciones, bonos, efectivo e inversiones alternativas. Una estrategia de asignación de activos bien diseñada puede ayudar a los inversores a alcanzar sus objetivos financieros mientras gestionan el riesgo y la volatilidad. Estos son algunos aspectos clave de la asignación de activos:

1. Equilibrio de riesgo y rendimiento: Las diferentes clases de activos tienen diferentes niveles de riesgo y rendimiento. Al asignar fondos a través de varias clases de activos, los inversores pueden lograr un equilibrio entre los rendimientos potenciales y la exposición al riesgo. Una cartera bien diversificada puede ayudar a los inversores a lograr los rendimientos deseados al tiempo que reduce la probabilidad de pérdidas significativas.

2. Estrategia a largo plazo: La asignación de activos es una estrategia de inversión a largo plazo que se centra en crear una cartera equilibrada y diversificada. Es esencial revisar y ajustar regularmente la

asignación para tener en cuenta los cambios en las condiciones del mercado, las circunstancias financieras personales y los objetivos de inversión.

3. Tolerancia al riesgo y horizonte de inversión: La tolerancia al riesgo y el horizonte de inversión de un inversor desempeñan un papel crucial en la determinación de la asignación adecuada de activos. Los inversores con una mayor tolerancia al riesgo y un horizonte de inversión más largo pueden asignar una mayor parte de su cartera a activos de mayor riesgo como acciones, mientras que aquellos con una menor tolerancia al riesgo y un horizonte de inversión más corto pueden favorecer activos más conservadores como bonos o efectivo.

4. Diversificación: La asignación de activos ayuda a los inversores a lograr la diversificación, que es la práctica de distribuir las inversiones en varias clases de activos para reducir el riesgo. La diversificación puede ayudar a mitigar el impacto de los activos de bajo rendimiento en la cartera general y suavizar los rendimientos a lo largo del tiempo.

5. Reequilibrio: El reequilibrio regular de la cartera es un aspecto crítico para mantener la asignación de activos deseada. Con el tiempo, el rendimiento de los activos individuales puede hacer que la asignación de la cartera se desvíe del objetivo, lo que

requiere un reequilibrio periódico mediante la venta de activos sobreponderados y la compra de activos infraponderados.

6. Gestión pasiva vs. gestión activa: Los inversores pueden abordar la asignación de activos a través de la gestión pasiva, utilizando fondos indexados o ETF para construir una cartera diversificada de bajo costo, o mediante una gestión activa, donde un gestor de cartera selecciona activamente las inversiones en un intento de superar al mercado. Ambas estrategias tienen sus pros y sus contras, y los inversores deben elegir el enfoque que mejor se adapte a sus necesidades y objetivos.

7. Asignación táctica de activos: Mientras que la asignación estratégica de activos se centra en la diversificación de la cartera a largo plazo, la asignación táctica de activos implica realizar ajustes a corto plazo en la cartera en función de las condiciones del mercado, las tendencias o las oportunidades de inversión. Este enfoque puede ayudar a los inversores a capitalizar las ineficiencias o cambios temporales del mercado, pero también puede requerir una gestión más activa y conllevar mayores riesgos.

La asignación de activos es un componente esencial de una estrategia de inversión exitosa, ya que puede ayudar a los inversores a equilibrar el riesgo y el rendimiento, lograr la diversificación y adaptar sus carteras a su tolerancia al riesgo y objetivos de inversión. Al considerar cuidadosamente sus objetivos y circunstancias financieras, los inversores pueden crear una cartera bien equilibrada y diversificada que pueda capear las fluctuaciones del mercado y ofrecer éxito a largo plazo.

5.2 Equilibrio entre riesgo y recompensa

Lograr el equilibrio adecuado entre riesgo y recompensa es un aspecto crucial de la inversión exitosa. Al seleccionar cuidadosamente las inversiones y diversificar su cartera, los inversores pueden gestionar el riesgo mientras persiguen sus objetivos financieros. Estos son algunos aspectos clave para equilibrar el riesgo y la recompensa:

1. Comprender el riesgo: El riesgo en la inversión se refiere a la incertidumbre de los rendimientos y el potencial de pérdidas. Las diferentes inversiones conllevan diferentes niveles de riesgo, y las inversiones de mayor riesgo suelen ofrecer mayores rendimientos potenciales. Los inversores deben evaluar los riesgos asociados con cada inversión y determinar su propia tolerancia al riesgo antes de tomar decisiones de inversión.

2. Compensación riesgo-rendimiento: La compensación riesgo-rendimiento es el principio de que los rendimientos potenciales más altos vienen con mayores riesgos. Al diversificar sus inversiones en varias clases de activos y valores individuales, los inversores pueden lograr un equilibrio entre riesgo y rendimiento, optimizando sus carteras para sus objetivos únicos y tolerancia al riesgo.

3. Tolerancia al riesgo: La tolerancia al riesgo de un inversor es su capacidad y voluntad de resistir las fluctuaciones en el valor de sus inversiones. Los factores que influyen en la tolerancia al riesgo incluyen el horizonte de inversión, los objetivos financieros y las circunstancias personales. Los inversores deben evaluar su tolerancia al riesgo y ajustar su asignación de activos en consecuencia para asegurarse de que se sienten cómodos con el nivel de riesgo en su cartera.

4. Diversificación: La diversificación es una estrategia clave para gestionar el riesgo y equilibrar las recompensas potenciales. Al invertir en una combinación de activos con diferentes niveles de riesgo y rendimiento, los inversores pueden crear una cartera que sea más resistente a las fluctuaciones del mercado y tenga un perfil de rendimiento más suave a lo largo del tiempo.

5. Correlación: La correlación se refiere al grado en que los rendimientos de diferentes inversiones se mueven juntos. Al incluir inversiones con correlación baja o negativa en su cartera, los inversores pueden reducir aún más el riesgo y mejorar la diversificación.

6. Rendimientos ajustados al riesgo: Los

rendimientos ajustados al riesgo tienen en cuenta tanto el rendimiento como el riesgo asociado con una inversión. Métricas como el ratio de Sharpe, que mide el rendimiento ajustado al riesgo de una inversión, pueden ayudar a los inversores a comparar inversiones e identificar aquellas que proporcionan el mejor equilibrio de riesgo y recompensa.

7. Monitoreo y reequilibrio: Monitorear regularmente el rendimiento de las inversiones individuales y la cartera general es esencial para mantener el equilibrio deseado entre riesgo y recompensa. A medida que cambian las condiciones del mercado y las inversiones funcionan de manera diferente, los inversores pueden necesitar reequilibrar su cartera ajustando su asignación de activos para mantener su nivel de riesgo objetivo y sus objetivos de inversión.

Equilibrar el riesgo y la recompensa es un aspecto crucial de la inversión exitosa. Al comprender los riesgos asociados con diferentes inversiones, evaluar su tolerancia al riesgo y emplear estrategias de diversificación y gestión de riesgos, los inversores pueden crear una cartera bien equilibrada que ofrezca una combinación óptima de riesgo y recompensa, posicionándolos para el éxito a largo plazo.

5.3 Rotación sectorial para un crecimiento constante

La rotación sectorial es una estrategia de inversión que implica cambiar la asignación de una cartera entre varios sectores de la economía en respuesta a las condiciones cambiantes del mercado y los ciclos económicos. Este enfoque tiene como objetivo capitalizar las diferentes características de crecimiento y rendimiento de cada sector, generando en última instancia un crecimiento constante y reduciendo el riesgo general de la cartera. Estos son algunos aspectos clave de la rotación sectorial:

1. Ciclos económicos: La economía se mueve a través de diferentes ciclos, como expansión, pico, contracción y valle. Cada fase del ciclo económico tiene efectos variables en diferentes sectores, con algunos sectores superando durante etapas específicas. Al comprender la relación entre los ciclos económicos y el desempeño del sector, los inversores pueden ajustar la asignación de su cartera para beneficiarse de estas tendencias.

2. Sectores líderes, rezagados y coincidentes: Los sectores pueden clasificarse como líderes, rezagados o coincidentes dependiendo de su desempeño en relación con el mercado general y el ciclo económico. Los sectores líderes tienden a superar al mercado al

principio de un ciclo económico, mientras que los sectores rezagados tienen un rendimiento inferior hasta las últimas etapas del ciclo. El desempeño de los sectores coincidentes generalmente rastrea el mercado general.

3. Diversificación: La rotación sectorial contribuye a la diversificación de la cartera al distribuir las inversiones en varios sectores con diferentes características de riesgo y rendimiento. Este enfoque puede ayudar a reducir la volatilidad de la cartera y proporcionar rendimientos más consistentes a lo largo del tiempo.

4. Gestión activa: La rotación sectorial requiere una gestión activa y una comprensión profunda de los ciclos económicos y el rendimiento del sector. Los inversores deben monitorear regularmente los indicadores económicos, las tendencias del mercado y el desempeño del sector para tomar decisiones de asignación bien informadas.

5. Fondos cotizados en bolsa (ETF): Los ETF pueden ser una herramienta eficaz para implementar una estrategia de rotación sectorial. Los inversores pueden ajustar fácilmente su exposición a diferentes sectores negociando ETF específicos del sector, lo que permite una mayor flexibilidad y menores costos de transacción en comparación con la compra y venta

de acciones individuales.

6. Tiempo y riesgos: La ejecución exitosa de una estrategia de rotación sectorial requiere un calendario preciso y una comprensión profunda de las tendencias económicas y del mercado. Las decisiones de asignación sectorial mal programadas pueden conducir a un rendimiento insuficiente y a un mayor riesgo. Además, las estrategias de rotación sectorial pueden tener un rendimiento inferior durante períodos de turbulencia del mercado o cuando el rendimiento del sector se desvía de los patrones históricos.

7. Evaluación del desempeño: El monitoreo del desempeño de una estrategia de rotación sectorial es esencial para garantizar que el enfoque logre los resultados deseados. Los inversores deben revisar periódicamente el rendimiento de sus asignaciones sectoriales, haciendo los ajustes necesarios para mantener su nivel de riesgo objetivo y sus objetivos de inversión.

La rotación sectorial es una estrategia de inversión proactiva que tiene como objetivo generar un crecimiento constante y reducir el riesgo mediante el ajuste de las asignaciones de cartera en respuesta a las condiciones cambiantes del mercado y los ciclos económicos. Al comprender la relación entre los ciclos económicos y el desempeño del sector, los inversores pueden aprovechar este enfoque para crear una cartera diversificada y resistente que esté bien posicionada para el éxito a largo plazo.

5.4 Invertir en acciones internacionales

Las acciones internacionales brindan a los inversores la oportunidad de diversificar aún más sus carteras y capitalizar el potencial de crecimiento de las economías fuera de su país de origen. Invertir en acciones internacionales puede ofrecer varios beneficios, pero también conlleva riesgos y desafíos únicos. Estos son algunos aspectos clave de la inversión en acciones internacionales:

1. Diversificación: Invertir en acciones internacionales permite a los inversores acceder a una gama más amplia de industrias, empresas y oportunidades de crecimiento, reduciendo la concentración de la cartera y mejorando potencialmente los rendimientos. La exposición a diferentes mercados y ciclos económicos puede ayudar a mitigar los riesgos asociados con un solo país o región.

2. Oportunidades de crecimiento: Los mercados emergentes y en desarrollo a menudo presentan un mayor potencial de crecimiento que los mercados maduros debido a factores como el crecimiento de la población, el aumento de la demanda de los consumidores y el aumento del gasto en infraestructura. Al invertir en acciones internacionales, los inversores pueden

aprovechar estas oportunidades de crecimiento y potencialmente lograr mayores rendimientos.

3. Riesgo cambiario: Invertir en acciones internacionales expone a los inversores al riesgo cambiario, ya que las fluctuaciones en los tipos de cambio pueden afectar el valor de las inversiones extranjeras. Si bien los movimientos de divisas a veces pueden mejorar los rendimientos, también pueden conducir a pérdidas. Los inversores deben ser conscientes de este riesgo y considerar estrategias para mitigarlo, como la cobertura de divisas.

4. Riesgo político y económico: Las acciones internacionales están sujetas a riesgos políticos y económicos exclusivos de los países en los que operan. Estos riesgos pueden incluir inestabilidad política, recesiones económicas, cambios en las regulaciones y restricciones comerciales. Los inversores deben investigar cuidadosamente el entorno político y económico de los países en los que invierten y estar preparados para ajustar sus carteras si las condiciones cambian.

5. Consideraciones fiscales: Invertir en acciones internacionales puede tener implicaciones fiscales, como la retención de impuestos sobre dividendos o impuestos sobre las ganancias de capital. Los inversores deben consultar con un profesional

de impuestos para comprender las implicaciones fiscales de sus inversiones internacionales y aprovechar cualquier tratado o crédito fiscal que pueda aplicarse.

6. Acceso a acciones internacionales: Los inversores pueden acceder a acciones internacionales a través de diversos métodos, como comprar acciones directamente en bolsas de valores extranjeras, invertir en American Depositary Receipts (ADR) o usar fondos mutuos y fondos cotizados en bolsa (ETF) que se centran en los mercados internacionales. Cada enfoque tiene sus ventajas y desventajas, y los inversores deben considerar cuidadosamente el mejor método para sus necesidades y objetivos.

7. Investigación y análisis: Investigar y analizar las acciones internacionales puede ser más desafiante que las acciones nacionales debido a factores como las barreras del idioma, la información limitada y las diferencias en las normas contables. Los inversores deben estar preparados para dedicar tiempo y recursos adicionales para llevar a cabo una investigación y análisis exhaustivos de las inversiones internacionales.

Invertir en acciones internacionales puede ofrecer beneficios significativos en términos de diversificación, potencial de crecimiento y exposición a diferentes mercados y ciclos económicos. Sin embargo, los inversores también deben ser conscientes de los riesgos y desafíos únicos asociados con la inversión internacional y considerar cuidadosamente sus estrategias de inversión y técnicas de gestión de riesgos para maximizar los beneficios potenciales y minimizar los riesgos potenciales.

Capítulo 6: Dominar la psicología del mercado

6.1 Superar los sesgos comunes de los inversores

Los sesgos de los inversores pueden afectar significativamente la toma de decisiones y el rendimiento de la inversión. Al reconocer y superar estos sesgos, los inversores pueden tomar decisiones más informadas y potencialmente mejorar sus resultados de inversión. Aquí hay algunos sesgos comunes de los inversores y estrategias para superarlos:

1. Sesgo de confirmación: El sesgo de confirmación ocurre cuando los inversores buscan y prestan más atención a la información que respalda sus creencias existentes mientras ignoran la evidencia contradictoria. Para superar el sesgo de confirmación, los inversores deben buscar activamente opiniones diversas e información contradictoria, desafiando sus propias suposiciones y creencias.

2. Sesgo de exceso de confianza: El sesgo de exceso de confianza se refiere a la tendencia de un inversor a sobreestimar sus propias habilidades y la precisión de sus predicciones. Para combatir el

exceso de confianza, los inversores deben mantener una actitud humilde, reconocer los límites de su conocimiento y estar abiertos a aprender de los demás y de sus propios errores.

3. Sesgo de anclaje: El sesgo de anclaje ocurre cuando los inversores confían demasiado en una información inicial (el "ancla") al tomar decisiones. Para superar el sesgo de anclaje, los inversores deben considerar una gama más amplia de datos y estar dispuestos a ajustar sus expectativas y valoraciones a medida que se disponga de nueva información.

4. Aversión a la pérdida: La aversión a la pérdida es la tendencia de los inversores a ser más sensibles a las pérdidas que a las ganancias, lo que puede llevar a una toma de decisiones subóptima, como mantener las inversiones perdidas demasiado tiempo o vender las inversiones ganadoras demasiado pronto. Para combatir la aversión a las pérdidas, los inversores deben centrarse en el rendimiento a largo plazo de su cartera y tomar decisiones basadas en sus objetivos y estrategia de inversión generales.

5. Mentalidad de rebaño: La mentalidad de rebaño se refiere a la tendencia de los inversores a seguir las acciones del mercado en general o de sus pares, lo que a menudo resulta en decisiones irracionales y burbujas de mercado. Para superar la mentalidad de

rebaño, los inversores deben mantener un enfoque de inversión disciplinado, realizar investigaciones independientes y evitar tomar decisiones basadas únicamente en el sentimiento o las tendencias del mercado.

6. Sesgo de recencia: El sesgo de recencia ocurre cuando los inversores dan más peso a los eventos e información recientes que a los datos históricos, lo que lleva al cortoplacismo y a la toma de decisiones reactiva. Para contrarrestar el sesgo de actualidad, los inversores deben centrarse en las tendencias a largo plazo y los datos históricos, y evitar tomar decisiones impulsivas basadas en eventos recientes del mercado.

7. Falacia del costo hundido: La falacia del costo hundido se refiere a la tendencia de los inversores a continuar invirtiendo en una posición perdedora debido a los recursos (tiempo, dinero) ya invertidos. Para evitar la falacia del costo hundido, los inversores deben evaluar objetivamente cada inversión en función de su potencial actual y futuro, en lugar de centrarse en las inversiones pasadas.

Al reconocer y abordar estos sesgos comunes de los inversores, las personas pueden tomar decisiones de inversión más racionales e informadas, mejorando en última instancia su rendimiento de inversión y ayudándoles a alcanzar sus objetivos financieros.

6.2 Navegar por la volatilidad del mercado

La volatilidad del mercado es una parte inherente de la inversión y puede conducir a fluctuaciones significativas en el valor de una cartera de inversiones. Navegar con éxito la volatilidad del mercado es esencial para el éxito de la inversión a largo plazo. Aquí hay algunas estrategias para ayudar a los inversores a gestionar la volatilidad del mercado:

1. Mantener una perspectiva a largo plazo: Los inversores deben centrarse en sus objetivos de inversión a largo plazo y evitar reaccionar impulsivamente a las fluctuaciones del mercado a corto plazo. Al mantener una perspectiva a largo plazo, los inversores pueden capear mejor la volatilidad del mercado y evitar tomar decisiones basadas en el miedo o la codicia.

2. Diversificación: La diversificación es una estrategia clave para gestionar la volatilidad del mercado. Al invertir en una combinación de activos con diferentes niveles de riesgo y rendimiento, los inversores pueden crear una cartera más resistente que sea menos susceptible a grandes oscilaciones de valor.

3. Reequilibre regularmente su cartera: revisar y

ajustar periódicamente la asignación de activos en una cartera puede ayudar a los inversores a mantener el nivel deseado de riesgo y rendimiento. El reequilibrio puede implicar la venta de activos que han tenido un buen rendimiento y la compra de activos de bajo rendimiento, lo que ayuda a gestionar el riesgo y mantener la diversificación.

4. Promedio de costo en dólares: El promedio de costo en dólares es una estrategia que implica invertir regularmente una cantidad fija de dinero en una inversión en particular, independientemente de su precio actual. Este enfoque puede ayudar a los inversores a gestionar la volatilidad del mercado al garantizar que compren más acciones cuando los precios son bajos y menos acciones cuando los precios son altos, lo que podría reducir el costo total de su inversión a lo largo del tiempo.

5. Desarrolle un plan de inversión: Tener un plan de inversión claro y bien definido puede ayudar a los inversores a mantenerse enfocados en sus objetivos y evitar tomar decisiones impulsivas en respuesta a la volatilidad del mercado. Un plan de inversión debe describir los objetivos de un inversor, la tolerancia al riesgo, el horizonte temporal y las estrategias de inversión preferidas.

6. Maneje las emociones: La toma de decisiones

emocionales puede conducir a malas decisiones de inversión y exacerbar el impacto de la volatilidad del mercado. Los inversores deben esforzarse por mantener un enfoque disciplinado y objetivo para invertir, centrándose en los hechos y los datos en lugar de dejar que las emociones impulsen sus decisiones.

7. Busque asesoramiento profesional: Trabajar con un asesor financiero o profesional de inversiones puede ayudar a los inversores a navegar por la volatilidad del mercado y tomar decisiones más informadas. Los asesores pueden proporcionar orientación, experiencia y una perspectiva objetiva, ayudando a los inversores a mantenerse enfocados en sus objetivos a largo plazo y tomar decisiones racionales durante las condiciones turbulentas del mercado.

Al emplear estas estrategias, los inversores pueden navegar mejor por la volatilidad del mercado y mantener un enfoque disciplinado y a largo plazo para invertir. Esto, a su vez, puede ayudar a los inversores a alcanzar sus objetivos financieros y generar riqueza con el tiempo, incluso frente a las fluctuaciones del mercado.

6.3 El arte de la paciencia y la disciplina

La paciencia y la disciplina son cualidades esenciales para una inversión exitosa, lo que permite a los inversores mantenerse enfocados en sus objetivos a largo plazo y evitar ser influenciados por las fluctuaciones o emociones del mercado a corto plazo. Cultivar la paciencia y la disciplina puede conducir a una toma de decisiones más informada y, en última instancia, mejorar el rendimiento de la inversión. Aquí hay algunos consejos para desarrollar paciencia y disciplina en la inversión:

1. Establezca objetivos de inversión claros: Establecer objetivos de inversión claros, medibles y alcanzables puede ayudar a los inversores a mantener el enfoque y resistir la tentación de tomar decisiones impulsivas. Al tener un objetivo bien definido, los inversores pueden alinear mejor sus decisiones de inversión con sus objetivos a largo plazo.

2. Desarrolle un plan de inversión integral: Un plan de inversión bien pensado puede servir como una hoja de ruta para la inversión disciplinada. El plan debe describir la tolerancia al riesgo del inversor, el horizonte temporal, la asignación de activos y las estrategias de inversión preferidas. Al adherirse a este plan, los inversores pueden mantener la disciplina y evitar tomar decisiones basadas en

emociones o eventos de mercado a corto plazo.

3. Adopte una perspectiva a largo plazo: Adoptar una perspectiva de inversión a largo plazo puede ayudar a los inversores a mantenerse pacientes y evitar reaccionar impulsivamente a las fluctuaciones del mercado. Centrarse en el potencial a largo plazo de las inversiones, en lugar de las ganancias o pérdidas a corto plazo, puede fomentar la paciencia y la toma de decisiones racionales.

4. Evite la inversión emocional: Reconocer y manejar las emociones es fundamental para mantener la disciplina en la inversión. Los inversores deben esforzarse por tomar decisiones basadas en datos, análisis y su plan de inversión, en lugar de dejarse llevar por el miedo, la codicia u otras emociones.

5. Practique la revisión y el reequilibrio regulares de la cartera: revisar y reequilibrar periódicamente una cartera puede ayudar a los inversores a mantener el nivel deseado de riesgo y rendimiento, así como a mantener su plan de inversión en marcha. Este enfoque disciplinado también puede proporcionar oportunidades para evaluar y ajustar las estrategias de inversión según sea necesario.

6. Aprender de la experiencia y los errores: Los inversores exitosos aprenden continuamente de sus

experiencias y errores, refinando su enfoque de inversión y procesos de toma de decisiones. Al permanecer abiertos al aprendizaje y al crecimiento, los inversores pueden cultivar la paciencia y la disciplina y, en última instancia, convertirse en inversores más efectivos.

7. Busque apoyo y orientación: Crear una red de asesores, mentores o pares de confianza puede ayudar a los inversores a mantenerse disciplinados y enfocados en sus objetivos de inversión. Al compartir experiencias, ideas y consejos, los inversores pueden obtener una perspectiva valiosa y apoyo en su viaje hacia la inversión disciplinada.

Desarrollar paciencia y disciplina en la inversión es un proceso continuo que puede conducir a una toma de decisiones más informada y a un mejor rendimiento de la inversión. Al establecer objetivos claros, desarrollar un plan de inversión integral y mantener una perspectiva a largo plazo, los inversores pueden cultivar la paciencia y la disciplina necesarias para el éxito de la inversión a largo plazo.

6.4 Cultivar una mentalidad contraria

Una mentalidad contraria es un enfoque de inversión que implica ir en contra de las tendencias prevalecientes del mercado o las opiniones populares. Los inversores contrarios creen que la mayoría de los participantes del mercado pueden estar equivocados, y buscan oportunidades para capitalizar los activos mal valorados resultantes de la mentalidad de rebaño o la toma de decisiones emocionales. Cultivar una mentalidad contraria puede conducir a decisiones de inversión más informadas y rendimientos potencialmente más altos. Aquí hay algunos consejos para desarrollar un enfoque contrario a la inversión:

1. Realizar una investigación independiente: Los inversores contrarios confían en su propia investigación y análisis en lugar de seguir la opinión popular. Esto implica llevar a cabo una diligencia debida exhaustiva, examinar los estados financieros y evaluar las condiciones del mercado para identificar posibles oportunidades de inversión que otros pueden pasar por alto.

2. Desafiar las opiniones populares: Para cultivar una mentalidad contraria, los inversores deben estar abiertos a cuestionar creencias ampliamente sostenidas y considerar puntos de vista alternativos.

Esto puede ayudar a identificar las ineficiencias del mercado y descubrir oportunidades que otros pueden no ver.

3. Abrazar la incomodidad: Ir contra la multitud puede ser incómodo, pero los inversores contrarios deben aprender a aceptar esta incomodidad como una parte necesaria de su estrategia de inversión. Al sentirse cómodos con estar en minoría, los inversores contrarios pueden tomar decisiones basadas en sus propias convicciones en lugar de dejarse influir por el sentimiento del mercado.

4. Enfoque en el valor: Los inversores contrarios a menudo buscan inversiones infravaloradas que han sido pasadas por alto o mal entendidas por el mercado en general. Al centrarse en el valor, los opositores pueden identificar oportunidades con un potencial significativo de apreciación una vez que el mercado reconoce el verdadero valor de estos activos.

5. Sea paciente: Las estrategias contrarias a menudo requieren paciencia, ya que puede tomar tiempo para que el sentimiento del mercado cambie y para que las inversiones infravaloradas se aprecien. Los inversores deben estar preparados para mantener sus posiciones durante períodos prolongados y esperar a que se desarrolle su tesis de inversión.

6. Gestione el riesgo: Si bien la inversión contraria puede ofrecer oportunidades atractivas, también conlleva riesgos. Los inversores deben gestionar cuidadosamente su exposición al riesgo diversificando su cartera, estableciendo órdenes de stop-loss y manteniendo un enfoque disciplinado para comprar y vender.

7. Aprender de los opositores exitosos: Estudiar las estrategias y filosofías de los inversores contrarios exitosos, como Warren Buffett o Sir John Templeton, puede proporcionar información valiosa e inspiración para desarrollar una mentalidad contraria.

Al cultivar una mentalidad contraria, los inversores pueden tomar decisiones más informadas, identificar oportunidades infravaloradas y, potencialmente, lograr mayores rendimientos. Este enfoque requiere investigación independiente, paciencia y la voluntad de desafiar las opiniones populares, pero puede ser una estrategia gratificante para aquellos que son disciplinados y comprometidos con sus principios de inversión.

Capítulo 7: Sincronización del mercado

7.1 Identificación de los ciclos de mercado

Los ciclos del mercado son las fluctuaciones naturales que ocurren en los mercados financieros a lo largo del tiempo. Consisten en períodos de expansión (mercados alcistas) y contracción (mercados bajistas), impulsados por diversos factores económicos, geopolíticos y psicológicos. Identificar con éxito los ciclos del mercado puede ayudar a los inversores a tomar decisiones más informadas y potencialmente mejorar el rendimiento de sus inversiones. Aquí hay algunas estrategias para reconocer y comprender los ciclos del mercado:

1. Estudie los indicadores económicos: Los indicadores económicos, como el crecimiento del PIB, las tasas de desempleo, la inflación y el sentimiento del consumidor, pueden proporcionar información sobre la salud general de la economía y ayudar a los inversores a identificar los ciclos del mercado. Al monitorear estos indicadores, los inversores pueden comprender mejor el estado actual de la economía y anticipar posibles cambios en las condiciones del mercado.

2. Analice las tendencias del mercado : Los inversores deben analizar regularmente las tendencias del mercado, incluidos los movimientos de precios, el volumen de negociación y el sentimiento del mercado. Estas tendencias pueden ayudar a los inversores a identificar posibles puntos de inflexión en los ciclos del mercado y tomar decisiones más informadas sobre cuándo comprar o vender activos.

3. Comprender la psicología del mercado: Los ciclos del mercado a menudo están influenciados por la psicología y las emociones de los inversores, como el miedo y la codicia. Al comprender el papel que desempeñan las emociones en los movimientos del mercado, los inversores pueden anticipar mejor los ciclos del mercado y tomar decisiones de inversión más racionales.

4. Monitorear las tasas de interés: Las tasas de interés juegan un papel importante en los ciclos del mercado, ya que influyen en los costos de endeudamiento, el gasto del consumidor y la inversión empresarial. Vigilar las políticas de los bancos centrales y las tendencias de las tasas de interés puede ayudar a los inversores a medir el impacto potencial en las condiciones del mercado y anticipar los cambios en los ciclos del mercado.

5. Busque patrones: Los patrones históricos y los eventos recurrentes, como las tendencias estacionales, pueden proporcionar pistas sobre los ciclos del mercado. Si bien el rendimiento pasado no garantiza resultados futuros, comprender estos patrones puede ayudar a los inversores a tomar decisiones más informadas sobre cuándo entrar o salir del mercado.

6. Diversifique sus fuentes de información: Para obtener una visión integral de los ciclos del mercado, los inversores deben diversificar sus fuentes de información, incluidos los medios de comunicación, los analistas financieros y los informes económicos. Esto puede ayudar a los inversores a reunir una gama más amplia de perspectivas y tomar decisiones más informadas.

7. Prepárese para la incertidumbre: Si bien es crucial tratar de identificar los ciclos del mercado, también es esencial reconocer que sincronizar el mercado perfectamente es casi imposible. Los inversores deben estar preparados para la incertidumbre y seguir siendo flexibles en sus estrategias de inversión para adaptarse a las condiciones cambiantes del mercado.

Al identificar los ciclos del mercado y comprender

los factores que los impulsan, los inversores pueden tomar decisiones más informadas sobre cuándo comprar o vender activos. Esto puede ayudarles potencialmente a capitalizar las oportunidades del mercado y mejorar el rendimiento general de su inversión. Sin embargo, los inversores también deben reconocer los desafíos inherentes en el momento de la sincronización del mercado y mantener un enfoque disciplinado y a largo plazo para invertir.

7.2 El poder del promedio del costo en dólares

El promedio de costo en dólares (DCA) es una poderosa estrategia de inversión que implica invertir consistentemente una cantidad fija de dinero en un activo o mercado en particular a intervalos regulares, independientemente de las condiciones del mercado o las fluctuaciones de precios. Este enfoque disciplinado puede ayudar a los inversores a gestionar el riesgo, navegar por la volatilidad del mercado y, potencialmente, mejorar el rendimiento de la inversión a largo plazo. Estos son algunos beneficios clave del promedio del costo en dólares:

1. Reducir el impacto de la volatilidad del mercado: Al invertir regularmente a lo largo del tiempo, DCA ayuda a suavizar el impacto de las fluctuaciones del mercado en una cartera de inversiones. Esto puede facilitar que los inversores mantengan el rumbo durante los períodos de volatilidad del mercado y eviten tomar decisiones impulsivas basadas en movimientos de precios a corto plazo.

2. Eliminar la necesidad de sincronización del mercado: Tratar de cronometrar el mercado es notoriamente difícil, incluso para los inversores experimentados. DCA elimina la necesidad de sincronización del mercado al garantizar que los inversores inviertan constantemente en el mercado,

independientemente de si está al alza o a la baja.

3. Menor costo promedio por acción: Con DCA, los inversores compran más acciones cuando los precios son bajos y menos acciones cuando los precios son altos. Con el tiempo, esto puede resultar en un menor costo promedio por acción, lo que podría mejorar los rendimientos de la inversión.

4. Fomente la inversión disciplinada: El promedio de costo en dólares promueve un enfoque disciplinado y a largo plazo para invertir al alentar a los inversores a cumplir con un programa de inversión regular. Esto puede ayudar a los inversores a mantenerse enfocados en sus objetivos a largo plazo y evitar ser influenciados por las fluctuaciones o emociones del mercado.

5. Simplifique las decisiones de inversión: DCA puede simplificar las decisiones de inversión al eliminar la necesidad de tratar de cronometrar el mercado o predecir movimientos de precios a corto plazo. En cambio, los inversores pueden centrarse en invertir consistentemente una cantidad fija de dinero a lo largo del tiempo, lo que les permite construir riqueza gradualmente.

6. Promueva el ahorro regular: Al comprometerse con un programa de inversión regular, DCA puede

ayudar a los inversionistas a desarrollar el hábito de ahorrar e invertir constantemente. Esto puede conducir a la acumulación de riqueza a lo largo del tiempo y contribuir al logro de objetivos financieros a largo plazo.

La implementación de una estrategia de promedio de costo en dólares es relativamente simple y se puede aplicar a varios tipos de inversiones, incluidas acciones, fondos mutuos y fondos cotizados en bolsa (ETF). Al invertir constantemente una cantidad fija de dinero a intervalos regulares, los inversores pueden gestionar el riesgo, navegar por la volatilidad del mercado y potencialmente mejorar el rendimiento de su inversión a largo plazo. Sin embargo, es esencial recordar que DCA no garantiza ganancias ni protege contra pérdidas en un mercado en declive, y los inversores deben considerar cuidadosamente su tolerancia al riesgo y sus objetivos financieros antes de implementar esta estrategia.

7.3 Swing Trading para obtener beneficios a corto plazo

El swing trading es una estrategia de trading a corto plazo que implica mantener posiciones en acciones, ETF u otros activos durante unos días a varias semanas. El objetivo del swing trading es capitalizar las fluctuaciones de precios a corto plazo y generar ganancias más rápidamente que las estrategias de inversión a largo plazo. Aquí hay algunos elementos clave del swing trading y consejos para el éxito:

1. Análisis técnico: Los swing traders dependen en gran medida del análisis técnico, que implica estudiar gráficos y patrones de precios para identificar posibles puntos de entrada y salida. Los indicadores técnicos, como las medias móviles, el índice de fuerza relativa (RSI) y los patrones de velas, pueden ayudar a los operadores oscilantes a determinar cuándo comprar o vender activos en función de los movimientos de precios a corto plazo.

2. Gestión de riesgos: La gestión eficaz del riesgo es esencial para el éxito del swing trading. Los swing traders deben establecer órdenes de stop-loss para limitar las pérdidas potenciales, y arriesgar sólo un pequeño porcentaje de su capital de trading en cada operación. Esto puede ayudar a preservar el capital y garantizar que los operadores puedan permanecer

en el mercado incluso después de una serie de operaciones perdedoras.

3. Desarrolle un plan de trading: Un plan de trading bien definido es crucial para el éxito del swing trading. El plan debe describir criterios específicos de entrada y salida, reglas de gestión de riesgos y objetivos comerciales. Al adherirse a un plan de trading, los swing traders pueden mantener la disciplina y evitar tomar decisiones impulsivas basadas en las emociones o el ruido del mercado.

4. Manténgase informado: Los swing traders deben mantenerse informados sobre las noticias del mercado, los informes de ganancias y otros eventos que pueden influir en los movimientos de precios a corto plazo. Mantenerse actualizado sobre los desarrollos del mercado puede ayudar a los operadores a tomar decisiones mejor informadas y ajustar rápidamente sus estrategias comerciales cuando sea necesario.

5. Sea paciente y disciplinado: El swing trading exitoso requiere paciencia y disciplina. Los swing traders deben esperar las oportunidades adecuadas para presentarse y evitar el overtrading o tomar decisiones impulsivas basadas en las emociones. Apegarse a un plan de trading bien definido y mantener un enfoque disciplinado puede mejorar las

posibilidades de éxito en el swing trading.

6. Diversifique su cartera: Los swing traders deben diversificar su cartera negociando una variedad de activos y sectores. Esto puede ayudar a distribuir el riesgo y proporcionar más oportunidades comerciales, aumentando las posibilidades de capturar operaciones rentables.

7. Aprender y mejorar continuamente: El swing trading es una habilidad que requiere un aprendizaje y mejora constantes. Los operadores deben revisar regularmente su rendimiento comercial, aprender de sus errores y refinar sus estrategias para ser más efectivos con el tiempo.

El swing trading puede ser una estrategia rentable para aquellos que están dispuestos a invertir el tiempo y el esfuerzo para dominar las habilidades y la disciplina necesarias. Sin embargo, es esencial recordar que el comercio a corto plazo implica mayores riesgos en comparación con la inversión a largo plazo, y los operadores deben considerar cuidadosamente su tolerancia al riesgo y sus objetivos financieros antes de participar en el swing trading.

7.4 Utilización de objetivos de stop loss y profit

Con el fin de gestionar eficazmente el riesgo y proteger las ganancias en las estrategias comerciales a corto y largo plazo, es importante utilizar los objetivos de stop loss y profit. Estas herramientas pueden ayudar a los inversores a mantener la disciplina, limitar las pérdidas potenciales y asegurar las ganancias cuando se producen movimientos de precios favorables. Aquí hay algunas ideas clave sobre el uso de stop loss y objetivos de ganancias:

1. Órdenes de stop loss: Una orden de stop loss es una instrucción para vender un activo cuando alcanza un cierto nivel de precio, limitando efectivamente la pérdida potencial del inversor en una operación. Las órdenes de stop loss son cruciales para la gestión de riesgos, ya que ayudan a proteger el capital comercial y evitan que las pérdidas se salgan de control.

- Establecer niveles razonables de stop loss: Al establecer órdenes de stop loss, los inversores deben considerar la volatilidad del activo, las fluctuaciones históricas de precios y su propia tolerancia al riesgo. Establecer stop loss demasiado ajustado puede resultar en que se detenga prematuramente de una operación, mientras que establecerlos demasiado amplios puede exponer a los inversores a pérdidas excesivas.

2. Objetivos de ganancias: Un objetivo de ganancias es un nivel de precio predeterminado en el que un inversor planea vender un activo para asegurar las ganancias. Establecer objetivos de ganancias puede ayudar a los inversores a mantener la disciplina y evitar aferrarse a una operación ganadora durante demasiado tiempo, lo que podría resultar en una pérdida de ganancias.

- Considere las relaciones riesgo-recompensa: Al establecer objetivos de ganancias, los inversores deben considerar la relación riesgo-recompensa de sus operaciones. Esta relación compara el beneficio potencial de una operación con la pérdida potencial, ayudando a los inversores a determinar si vale la pena realizar una operación. Una relación riesgo-recompensa favorable (por ejemplo, 2:1 o superior) puede mejorar las posibilidades de éxito comercial a largo plazo.

3. Trailing Stop Loss: Un trailing stop loss es una orden dinámica de stop loss que se mueve con el precio del activo, bloqueando las ganancias a medida que aumenta el precio y al mismo tiempo proporciona protección contra una reversión repentina. Trailing stop loss puede ser una forma efectiva de asegurar ganancias en mercados de tendencia sin salir prematuramente de una

operación.

4. Adaptación de los objetivos de stop loss y profit: Las condiciones del mercado y los precios de los activos pueden cambiar rápidamente, por lo que es esencial que los inversores reevalúen regularmente sus niveles objetivo de stop loss y profit. Ajustar estos niveles en función de la nueva información o la dinámica cambiante del mercado puede ayudar a optimizar la gestión de riesgos y las estrategias de toma de beneficios.

5. Utilice los objetivos de stop loss y profit de manera consistente: Para gestionar eficazmente el riesgo y proteger las ganancias, los inversores deben aplicar consistentemente estrategias de stop loss y profit target a todas sus operaciones. Este enfoque disciplinado puede ayudar a minimizar las pérdidas y maximizar las ganancias a lo largo del tiempo.

Al utilizar objetivos de stop loss y ganancias, los inversores pueden administrar mejor el riesgo y proteger su capital comercial, al tiempo que bloquean las ganancias cuando se producen movimientos de precios favorables. Estas herramientas pueden ser valiosas tanto para los operadores a corto plazo como para los inversores a largo plazo, ayudándoles a mantener la disciplina y mejorar el rendimiento general de su inversión.

Capítulo 8: Inversión inteligente desde el punto de vista fiscal

8.1 Comprensión de las ganancias y pérdidas de capital

Invertir en el mercado de valores puede tener implicaciones fiscales significativas, y comprender las ganancias y pérdidas de capital es esencial para una inversión inteligente desde el punto de vista fiscal. Las ganancias y pérdidas de capital son las ganancias o pérdidas obtenidas cuando se vende o enajena un activo. Administrar estas ganancias y pérdidas de manera efectiva puede ayudar a minimizar su obligación tributaria y maximizar sus rendimientos de inversión después de impuestos. Aquí hay algunos conceptos clave relacionados con las ganancias y pérdidas de capital:

1. Ganancias de capital: Una ganancia de capital ocurre cuando un activo se vende por un precio más alto que su precio de compra (también conocido como su base de costo). Las ganancias de capital generalmente están sujetas a impuestos, y la tasa impositiva depende del nivel de ingresos del inversionista y del período de tenencia del activo.

- Ganancias de capital a corto plazo: Las ganancias

de los activos mantenidos durante un año o menos se consideran ganancias de capital a corto plazo y se gravan a la tasa ordinaria del impuesto sobre la renta del inversor.

Ganancias de capital a largo plazo: Las ganancias de los activos mantenidos durante más de un año se consideran ganancias de capital a largo plazo y, por lo general, se gravan a una tasa más baja que las ganancias de capital a corto plazo, lo que hace que la inversión a largo plazo sea más eficiente desde el punto de vista fiscal.

2. Pérdidas de capital: Una pérdida de capital ocurre cuando un activo se vende por un precio más bajo que su precio de compra. Las pérdidas de capital se pueden utilizar para compensar las ganancias de capital, reduciendo la obligación fiscal general del inversor.

- Deducción por pérdida de capital: Si las pérdidas de capital exceden las ganancias de capital en un año fiscal determinado, los inversores generalmente pueden deducir hasta una cierta cantidad de la pérdida neta de sus ingresos imponibles, reduciendo aún más su obligación tributaria. Cualquier pérdida restante puede trasladarse para compensar las ganancias en años futuros.

3. Recolección de pérdidas fiscales: La recolección de pérdidas fiscales es una estrategia que implica la venta de activos de bajo rendimiento para realizar pérdidas de capital, que luego se pueden usar para compensar las ganancias de capital de otras inversiones. Esto puede ayudar a minimizar la responsabilidad tributaria del inversionista y potencialmente aumentar las declaraciones después de impuestos.

4. Mantenga registros: Los inversores deben mantener registros detallados de sus transacciones de inversión, incluidas las fechas de compra y venta, los precios y las tarifas. Estos registros serán esenciales para calcular con precisión las ganancias y pérdidas de capital y preparar declaraciones de impuestos.

5. Consulte a un profesional de impuestos: Las leyes tributarias pueden ser complejas y estar sujetas a cambios, por lo que es esencial consultar con un profesional de impuestos para garantizar el cumplimiento y optimizar las estrategias de ahorro de impuestos. Un asesor fiscal puede proporcionar orientación personalizada basada en su situación financiera específica y objetivos de inversión.

Al comprender las ganancias y pérdidas de capital

e implementar estrategias de inversión fiscalmente inteligentes, los inversores pueden minimizar su responsabilidad fiscal y maximizar sus rendimientos de inversión después de impuestos. Esto puede ser particularmente importante para los inversores a largo plazo, ya que el impacto de los impuestos en el rendimiento de la inversión puede ser significativo con el tiempo.

8.2 Maximizar la eficiencia fiscal

Maximizar la eficiencia fiscal es crucial para los inversores que buscan optimizar sus rendimientos después de impuestos. Al implementar estrategias de inversión eficientes desde el punto de vista fiscal, puede minimizar el impacto de los impuestos en sus inversiones y mantener más de sus ganancias duramente ganadas. Estos son algunos consejos para maximizar la eficiencia fiscal en su cartera de inversiones:

1. Mantener inversiones a largo plazo: Las ganancias de capital a largo plazo (de activos mantenidos durante más de un año) generalmente se gravan a una tasa más baja que las ganancias de capital a corto plazo. Mantener inversiones a largo plazo puede ayudarlo a aprovechar estas tasas impositivas preferenciales y reducir su obligación tributaria general.

2. Utilice cuentas con ventajas fiscales: Las cuentas con ventajas fiscales, como las cuentas de jubilación individual (IRA) y los planes 401 (k), pueden proporcionar beneficios fiscales significativos. Las contribuciones a estas cuentas pueden ser deducibles de impuestos, y las inversiones crecen con impuestos diferidos o libres de impuestos, dependiendo del tipo de cuenta. El uso de estas cuentas puede ayudarlo a

ahorrar en impuestos y maximizar los rendimientos de su inversión a largo plazo.

3. Considere los bonos municipales: Los ingresos por intereses de los bonos municipales generalmente están exentos del impuesto federal sobre la renta y, en algunos casos, también de los impuestos estatales y locales. Incluir bonos municipales en su cartera puede proporcionar ingresos libres de impuestos y ayudar a diversificar sus inversiones.

4. Recolección de pérdidas fiscales: Como se mencionó anteriormente, la recolección de pérdidas fiscales implica vender inversiones de bajo rendimiento para realizar pérdidas de capital, que luego se pueden usar para compensar las ganancias de capital de otras inversiones. Esta estrategia puede ayudar a reducir su obligación tributaria general y potencialmente aumentar sus declaraciones después de impuestos.

5. Invierta en fondos fiscalmente eficientes: Ciertos fondos mutuos y fondos cotizados en bolsa (ETF) están diseñados para minimizar las distribuciones imponibles mediante la gestión de sus carteras de una manera eficiente desde el punto de vista fiscal. Considere invertir en estos fondos fiscalmente eficientes para reducir el impacto de los impuestos en los rendimientos de su inversión.

6. Reequilibrio en cuentas con ventajas fiscales: Al reequilibrar su cartera, considere realizar transacciones dentro de cuentas con ventajas fiscales en lugar de cuentas imponibles. Esto puede ayudarlo a evitar desencadenar eventos imponibles, como ganancias de capital, cuando compra o vende inversiones.

7. Revise su cartera regularmente: revise regularmente su cartera de inversiones para asegurarse de que siga siendo eficiente desde el punto de vista fiscal y alineada con sus objetivos financieros. Esto puede implicar ajustar su asignación de activos, reequilibrar o implementar estrategias de recolección de pérdidas fiscales.

Al incorporar estas estrategias fiscalmente eficientes en su plan de inversión, puede minimizar el impacto de los impuestos en su cartera y maximizar sus rendimientos después de impuestos. Es esencial consultar con un profesional de impuestos o asesor financiero para garantizar el cumplimiento de las leyes fiscales y recibir orientación personalizada adaptada a su situación financiera específica.

8.3 Cuentas de inversión con ventajas fiscales

Las cuentas de inversión con ventajas fiscales están diseñadas específicamente para ofrecer beneficios fiscales que pueden ayudarlo a ahorrar para la jubilación, la educación u otras metas financieras a largo plazo. El uso de estas cuentas puede mejorar significativamente los rendimientos generales de su inversión al minimizar los impuestos sobre sus inversiones. Estas son algunas de las cuentas de inversión con ventajas fiscales más comunes:

1. Cuentas individuales de jubilación (IRA): Las IRA son cuentas de ahorro para la jubilación que ofrecen beneficios fiscales para ayudarlo a ahorrar para la jubilación. Hay dos tipos principales de IRA:

- IRA tradicional: Las contribuciones a una IRA tradicional pueden ser deducibles de impuestos, dependiendo de sus ingresos y participación en un plan de jubilación patrocinado por el empleador. Las ganancias de inversión crecen con impuestos diferidos, y los retiros en la jubilación se gravan como ingresos ordinarios.

- Roth IRA: Las contribuciones a una Roth IRA se realizan con dólares después de impuestos, y los retiros en la jubilación están libres de impuestos, siempre que se cumplan ciertas condiciones. Las ganancias de inversión también crecen libres de impuestos en una Roth IRA, lo que la convierte en una opción atractiva para aquellos que esperan estar en una categoría impositiva más alta en la jubilación.

2..Planes 401(k): Un 401(k) es un plan de ahorro para la jubilación patrocinado por el empleador que permite a los empleados contribuir con una parte de su salario antes de impuestos al plan. Las ganancias de inversión crecen con impuestos diferidos, y los retiros en la jubilación se gravan como ingresos ordinarios. Algunos empleadores también ofrecen opciones Roth 401 (k), que combinan características de los planes 401 (k) tradicionales y Roth IRA.

3. Planes 403(b) y 457: Estos planes son similares a los planes 401(k) pero están diseñados para empleados de instituciones educativas públicas, organizaciones sin fines de lucro y organizaciones gubernamentales. Al igual que los planes 401 (k), las contribuciones se realizan con dólares antes de impuestos, las ganancias de inversión crecen con impuestos diferidos y los retiros en la jubilación se gravan como ingresos ordinarios.

4. Planes de ahorro para la universidad 529: Un plan 529 es una cuenta de inversión con ventajas fiscales diseñada para ayudarlo a ahorrar para gastos educativos futuros. Las contribuciones a un plan 529

se hacen con dólares después de impuestos, y las ganancias de inversión crecen libres de impuestos. Los retiros para gastos de educación calificados, como matrícula, tarifas y libros de texto, también están libres de impuestos.

5. Cuentas de ahorro para la salud (HSA): Las HSA son cuentas con ventajas fiscales diseñadas para ayudarlo a ahorrar para gastos de atención médica. Las contribuciones a una HSA son deducibles de impuestos, las ganancias de inversión crecen libres de impuestos y los retiros por gastos médicos calificados están libres de impuestos. Las HSA están disponibles para las personas inscritas en un plan de salud con deducible alto (HDHP).

Al utilizar estas cuentas de inversión con ventajas fiscales, puede minimizar el impacto de los impuestos en los rendimientos de su inversión y lograr de manera más efectiva sus objetivos financieros a largo plazo. Asegúrese de consultar con un asesor financiero o profesional de impuestos para determinar qué cuentas con ventajas fiscales son apropiadas para su situación financiera y objetivos específicos.

8.4 Estrategias para la planificación fiscal de fin de año

La planificación fiscal de fin de año es una parte esencial de la gestión de su cartera de inversiones y la minimización de su obligación fiscal. La implementación de estrategias efectivas de planificación fiscal antes de fin de año puede ayudarlo a optimizar sus rendimientos de inversión después de impuestos y aprovechar los beneficios fiscales disponibles. Aquí hay algunas estrategias clave para la planificación fiscal de fin de año:

1. Revise su cartera de inversiones: Evalúe su cartera para identificar cualquier ganancia y pérdida de capital realizada, así como cualquier oportunidad potencial para la recolección de pérdidas fiscales. Este también es un buen momento para reequilibrar su cartera y asegurarse de que permanezca alineada con sus objetivos financieros y tolerancia al riesgo.

2. Recolección de pérdidas fiscales: Como se mencionó anteriormente, la recolección de pérdidas fiscales implica la venta de inversiones de bajo rendimiento para realizar pérdidas de capital, que luego se pueden usar para compensar las ganancias de capital de otras inversiones. Implementar esta estrategia antes de fin de año puede ayudar a reducir su obligación tributaria general para el año.

3. Maximice las contribuciones a las cuentas con ventajas fiscales: Asegúrese de haber contribuido con la cantidad máxima permitida a sus cuentas con ventajas fiscales, como IRA, 401 (k) y HSA. Estas contribuciones pueden reducir potencialmente su ingreso imponible y ayudarlo a ahorrar en impuestos.

4. Evalúe su categoría impositiva: Revise su ingreso imponible proyectado para el año y determine si está cerca de pasar a una categoría impositiva más alta o más baja. Dependiendo de su situación, es posible que desee acelerar o diferir ciertos ingresos o deducciones para optimizar su situación fiscal.

5. Considere las donaciones caritativas: Hacer donaciones caritativas antes de fin de año puede proporcionar beneficios fiscales, ya que las donaciones a organizaciones benéficas calificadas pueden ser deducibles de impuestos. Asegúrese de mantener registros de sus donaciones y consulte a un profesional de impuestos para asegurarse de que está maximizando sus deducciones.

6. Planifique las distribuciones mínimas requeridas (RMD): Si tiene 72 años o más y tiene una cuenta IRA tradicional u otra cuenta de jubilación con impuestos diferidos, generalmente se le exige que

tome una distribución mínima de la cuenta cada año. Asegúrese de tomar su RMD antes de fin de año para evitar posibles multas fiscales.

7. Evalúe las opciones de inversión fiscalmente eficientes: considere invertir en vehículos de inversión eficientes desde el punto de vista fiscal, como bonos municipales libres de impuestos o fondos mutuos y ETF administrados por impuestos, para ayudar a reducir el impacto de los impuestos en los rendimientos de su inversión.

8. Consulte a un profesional de impuestos: La planificación fiscal de fin de año puede ser compleja y las leyes fiscales están sujetas a cambios. Consulte con un profesional de impuestos para asegurarse de que está aprovechando todos los beneficios fiscales disponibles e implementando las estrategias más efectivas para su situación financiera específica.

Al implementar estas estrategias de planificación fiscal de fin de año, puede optimizar sus rendimientos de inversión después de impuestos y minimizar su obligación tributaria. Asegúrese de consultar con un asesor financiero o profesional de impuestos para recibir orientación personalizada adaptada a su situación financiera y objetivos específicos.

Capítulo 9: Construyendo riqueza a través de ingresos pasivos

9.1 El poder de la reinversión de dividendos

La reinversión de dividendos es una estrategia poderosa que puede mejorar significativamente los rendimientos de su inversión a largo plazo y ayudarlo a generar riqueza a través de ingresos pasivos. Al reinvertir los dividendos, puede aprovechar el efecto capitalizado, que permite que sus inversiones crezcan a un ritmo acelerado con el tiempo. Así es como funciona la reinversión de dividendos y por qué es una parte esencial de una estrategia de ingresos pasivos:

1. Entender los dividendos: Los dividendos son pagos realizados por las empresas a sus accionistas como una forma de distribuir una parte de sus ganancias. Las acciones que pagan dividendos pueden proporcionar un flujo constante de ingresos para los inversores, que pueden usarse para gastos de subsistencia, reinvertirse o guardarse para uso futuro.

2. Reinversión de dividendos: En lugar de tomar dividendos en efectivo, la reinversión de dividendos implica usar los pagos de dividendos para comprar

acciones adicionales de las acciones. Esto se puede hacer automáticamente a través de un plan de reinversión de dividendos (DRIP) o reinvirtiendo manualmente los ingresos de los dividendos.

3. Efecto compuesto: El poder de la reinversión de dividendos radica en el efecto compuesto. A medida que reinvierte sus dividendos, está aumentando efectivamente el número de acciones que posee, lo que a su vez genera más dividendos en el futuro. Con el tiempo, esto crea un efecto de bola de nieve, permitiendo que sus inversiones crezcan a un ritmo acelerado y potencialmente conducen a rendimientos sustanciales a largo plazo.

4. Beneficios de la reinversión de dividendos:

 - Crecimiento acelerado de la cartera: La reinversión de dividendos puede ayudarlo a hacer crecer su cartera de inversiones más rápidamente, ya que el efecto compuesto permite que sus inversiones aumenten exponencialmente con el tiempo.

 - Promedio de costo en dólares: La reinversión de dividendos le permite aprovechar el promedio de costo en dólares, ya que está comprando constantemente acciones adicionales a varios puntos de precio. Esto puede ayudar a reducir el impacto de la volatilidad del mercado en sus inversiones.

Creación de riqueza a largo plazo: Al reinvertir los dividendos y aprovechar el poder de la capitalización, puede generar una riqueza sustancial a largo plazo y generar un flujo de ingresos pasivo que puede ayudarlo a alcanzar sus objetivos financieros.

- Eficiencia fiscal: En algunos casos, reinvertir dividendos puede ser más eficiente desde el punto de vista fiscal que tomar dividendos en efectivo, ya que puede diferir los impuestos sobre los dividendos reinvertidos hasta que venda las acciones.

5. Implementación de la reinversión de dividendos: Para comenzar a reinvertir dividendos, puede inscribirse en un DRIP ofrecido por la compañía o su corretaje, o puede reinvertir dividendos manualmente comprando acciones adicionales de las acciones. Asegúrese de consultar con un asesor financiero o profesional de impuestos para asegurarse de que está implementando una estrategia de reinversión de dividendos que se alinee con sus metas y objetivos financieros específicos.

Al utilizar el poder de la reinversión de dividendos, puede crear un flujo de ingresos pasivo que crece con el tiempo, ayudándole a construir riqueza a largo plazo y alcanzar sus objetivos financieros.

9.2 Fideicomisos de inversión inmobiliaria (REIT)

Los Fideicomisos de Inversión Inmobiliaria (REIT) son una opción atractiva para los inversores que buscan generar ingresos pasivos y diversificar su cartera de inversiones. Los REIT son compañías que poseen, administran o financian propiedades inmobiliarias que generan ingresos, lo que permite a los inversores ganar una parte de los ingresos por alquiler y la apreciación de la propiedad. Aquí hay una descripción general de los REIT y sus beneficios para los inversores de ingresos pasivos:

1. Tipos de REIT: Los REIT se pueden clasificar en varios tipos, según las propiedades que poseen y sus estrategias de inversión:

- REIT de capital: Estos REIT poseen y administran propiedades generadoras de ingresos, como edificios de apartamentos, edificios de oficinas, centros comerciales y hoteles. Los REIT de capital generan ingresos principalmente a través del cobro de alquileres y la apreciación de la propiedad.

- REIT hipotecarios: Estos REIT invierten en hipotecas o valores respaldados por hipotecas, generando ingresos a través del pago de intereses en sus carteras de préstamos.

- REIT híbridos: Estos REIT combinan elementos de REIT de capital e hipotecarios, invirtiendo tanto en propiedades como en hipotecas.

2. Beneficios de invertir en REIT:

- Ingresos pasivos: Los REIT están obligados por ley a distribuir al menos el 90% de sus ingresos imponibles a los accionistas en forma de dividendos, lo que los convierte en una opción atractiva para los inversores que buscan un flujo constante de ingresos pasivos.

- Diversificación: Invertir en REIT le permite diversificar su cartera de inversiones al agregar exposición al sector inmobiliario, lo que puede ayudar a reducir el riesgo general de la cartera.

- Liquidez: Los REIT que cotizan en bolsa se compran y venden en las principales bolsas de valores, proporcionando liquidez y facilidad de negociación en comparación con las inversiones inmobiliarias directas.

- Gestión profesional: Los REIT son administrados por profesionales experimentados que supervisan la adquisición, administración y financiamiento de propiedades, lo que le permite beneficiarse de su experiencia sin la molestia de administrar inversiones inmobiliarias usted mismo.

3. Cómo invertir en REITs: Hay varias maneras de invertir en REITs, incluyendo:

- Compra directa de acciones de REIT individuales en una bolsa de valores.

- Invertir en fondos mutuos REIT o fondos cotizados en bolsa (ETF), que proporcionan exposición a una cartera diversificada de REIT.

- Invertir en fondos indexados o ETF centrados en bienes raíces, que pueden incluir REIT como parte de sus tenencias.

Al invertir en REIT, es esencial realizar una investigación exhaustiva y la debida diligencia para asegurarse de que está eligiendo REIT de alta calidad con equipos de gestión sólidos, carteras de propiedades diversificadas y un historial de generación de ingresos constante. Asegúrese de consultar con un asesor financiero para determinar si los REIT son una adición adecuada a su cartera de inversiones y cómo pueden ayudarlo a alcanzar sus objetivos de ingresos pasivos.

9.3 Sociedades limitadas maestras (MLP)

Las sociedades limitadas maestras (MLP) son un tipo único de vehículo de inversión que puede brindar a los inversores la oportunidad de generar ingresos pasivos mientras se benefician de las ventajas fiscales de una estructura de asociación. Los MLP están involucrados principalmente en el sector energético, centrándose en el transporte, almacenamiento y procesamiento de recursos naturales como el petróleo y el gas natural. Aquí hay una descripción general de los MLP y sus beneficios potenciales para los inversores de ingresos pasivos:

1. Comprender los MLP: Los MLP son asociaciones que cotizan en bolsa que emiten unidades en lugar de acciones. Como partícipe, se le considera un socio limitado en el MLP, lo que le da derecho a una parte de los ingresos, deducciones y beneficios fiscales de la sociedad.

2. Ventajas fiscales: Uno de los principales atractivos de los MLP es su estructura fiscal. A diferencia de las corporaciones, los MLP no están sujetos a doble imposición. En cambio, los ingresos de la sociedad solo se gravan a nivel de socio individual. Esto significa que los MLP a menudo pueden distribuir un mayor porcentaje de sus ingresos a los partícipes en comparación con las corporaciones, lo que puede

resultar en mayores rendimientos.

3. Ingresos pasivos: Los MLP son conocidos por sus rendimientos de distribución consistentes y, a menudo, atractivos, lo que los convierte en una opción popular entre los inversores que buscan ingresos. Los ingresos generados por los MLP provienen principalmente de contratos estables y a largo plazo en el sector energético, proporcionando una fuente confiable de flujo de efectivo.

4. Diversificación: Invertir en MLP puede ayudar a diversificar su cartera de inversiones al proporcionar exposición al sector energético, que a menudo tiene una baja correlación con otras clases de activos. Esto puede ayudar a reducir el riesgo general de su cartera.

5. Cómo invertir en MLP: Hay varias maneras de invertir en MLP, que incluyen:

- Compra directa de unidades MLP en una bolsa de valores.

- Invertir en fondos mutuos enfocados en MLP o fondos cotizados en bolsa (ETF), que proporcionan exposición a una cartera diversificada de MLP.

- Invertir en fondos cerrados de MLP, que son carteras gestionadas activamente de MLP que cotizan en bolsas de valores.

Al invertir en MLP, es esencial considerar las posibles implicaciones fiscales y los requisitos de información asociados con estas inversiones. Los partícipes de MLP deben informar su parte de los ingresos, deducciones y créditos fiscales de la sociedad en sus declaraciones de impuestos personales, lo que puede aumentar la complejidad de su declaración de impuestos. Asegúrese de consultar con un asesor financiero o profesional de impuestos para determinar si los MLP son una adición adecuada a su cartera de inversiones y cómo pueden ayudarlo a alcanzar sus objetivos de ingresos pasivos.

9.4 Plataformas de préstamos peer-to-peer

Las plataformas de préstamos peer-to-peer (P2P) son una forma innovadora de generar ingresos pasivos al proporcionar préstamos a individuos o empresas que necesitan financiamiento. Estas plataformas conectan a los prestatarios con inversores que están dispuestos a prestar dinero a cambio de pagos de intereses. Aquí hay una descripción general de las plataformas de préstamos P2P y sus beneficios potenciales para los inversores de ingresos pasivos:

1. Comprender los préstamos P2P: Las plataformas de préstamos P2P actúan como intermediarios entre prestatarios e inversores, facilitando el proceso de préstamo y manejando la suscripción, el reembolso y los cobros de préstamos. Como inversionista, puede optar por prestar dinero a una variedad de prestatarios con diferentes perfiles de crédito, propósitos de préstamo y tasas de interés, lo que le permite personalizar su cartera de inversiones en función de su tolerancia al riesgo y objetivos de ingresos.

2. Beneficios potenciales de los préstamos P2P:

- Rendimientos atractivos: Los préstamos P2P pueden ofrecer mayores rendimientos en comparación con las inversiones tradicionales de renta fija, como bonos o cuentas de ahorro, debido a las tasas de interés más altas que se cobran a los prestatarios.

- Diversificación: Invertir en préstamos P2P puede ayudar a diversificar su cartera de inversiones al proporcionar exposición a una clase de activos alternativos que pueden tener una baja correlación con las inversiones tradicionales como acciones y bonos.

- Personalización: Las plataformas de préstamos P2P le permiten seleccionar préstamos individuales en función de su tolerancia al riesgo, rendimientos deseados y criterios de inversión, lo que le permite crear una cartera de inversiones personalizada que se alinea con sus objetivos financieros.

3. Riesgos asociados con los préstamos P2P:

- Riesgo de incumplimiento: los préstamos P2P no están garantizados, lo que significa que no hay garantía para respaldar el préstamo en caso de que el prestatario incumpla. Como resultado, el principal riesgo asociado con los préstamos P2P es la posibilidad de incumplimiento del prestatario, lo que podría conducir a una pérdida de su capital invertido.

- Riesgo de liquidez: Los préstamos P2P no son tan líquidos como las inversiones tradicionales como acciones o bonos, que se pueden comprar y vender fácilmente en las bolsas de valores. Si bien algunas plataformas de préstamos P2P ofrecen mercados secundarios para préstamos comerciales, no hay garantía de que pueda vender sus préstamos rápidamente o al precio deseado.

4. Cómo comenzar con los préstamos P2P: Para comenzar a invertir en préstamos P2P, puede registrarse para obtener una cuenta con una plataforma de préstamos P2P de buena reputación, como LendingClub, Prosper o Funding Circle. Una vez que su cuenta esté configurada, puede buscar préstamos disponibles, revisar los perfiles de los prestatarios y elegir en qué préstamos invertir según sus criterios de inversión.

Antes de invertir en préstamos P2P, es esencial realizar una investigación exhaustiva y la debida diligencia en la plataforma de préstamos y los préstamos individuales que está considerando. Asegúrese de consultar con un asesor financiero para determinar si los préstamos P2P son una adición adecuada a su cartera de inversiones y cómo pueden ayudarlo a alcanzar sus objetivos de ingresos pasivos.

Capítulo 10: Mantenerse en el camino hacia la libertad financiera

10.1 Monitoreo y ajuste regular de su cartera

Lograr la libertad financiera a través de ingresos pasivos requiere un esfuerzo constante para monitorear y ajustar su cartera de inversiones. A medida que los mercados evolucionan y sus objetivos financieros cambian, es esencial reevaluar sus inversiones y hacer ajustes en consecuencia. En esta sección, discutiremos la importancia de monitorear y ajustar regularmente su cartera para mantenerse en el camino hacia la libertad financiera:

1. Revise el rendimiento de su inversión: Evalúe regularmente el rendimiento de sus inversiones para asegurarse de que estén en línea con sus objetivos financieros. Esto incluye comparar los rendimientos de sus inversiones con sus respectivos puntos de referencia, así como evaluar el rendimiento general de su cartera en relación con sus objetivos.

2. Reequilibre su cartera: Con el tiempo, la asignación de sus activos puede cambiar debido a las fluctuaciones en el rendimiento del mercado. Reequilibrar su cartera implica ajustar sus inversiones para mantener su asignación de activos

objetivo, lo que puede ayudar a controlar el riesgo y garantizar que su cartera permanezca alineada con su estrategia de inversión.

3. Reevalúe su tolerancia al riesgo: A medida que avanza a través de diferentes etapas de la vida, su tolerancia al riesgo puede cambiar. Reevaluar regularmente su tolerancia al riesgo puede ayudarlo a realizar los ajustes necesarios en su cartera para reflejar su situación financiera y sus objetivos actuales.

4. Actualice sus objetivos de inversión: Sus objetivos financieros pueden evolucionar con el tiempo, ya sea debido a cambios en sus circunstancias personales o cambios en sus prioridades. Revise y actualice periódicamente sus objetivos de inversión para asegurarse de que su cartera permanezca alineada con sus objetivos financieros a largo plazo.

5. Manténgase informado sobre las condiciones del mercado: Manténgase informado sobre las condiciones actuales del mercado y cualquier evento significativo que pueda afectar sus inversiones. Mantenerse al día sobre las tendencias y noticias del mercado puede ayudarlo a tomar decisiones informadas sobre el ajuste de su cartera y el aprovechamiento de nuevas oportunidades de inversión.

6. Consulte con un asesor financiero: consulte regularmente con un asesor financiero para analizar su cartera, estrategia de inversión y cualquier ajuste necesario para mantenerse en el camino hacia la libertad financiera. Un asesor financiero puede proporcionar información valiosa, orientación y recomendaciones basadas en su experiencia y conocimiento de los mercados.

Al monitorear y ajustar regularmente su cartera, puede asegurarse de que sus inversiones permanezcan alineadas con sus objetivos financieros y tolerancia al riesgo. Este enfoque proactivo lo ayudará a mantenerse en el camino para lograr la libertad financiera a través de ingresos pasivos y mantener su estilo de vida deseado a largo plazo.

10.2 Navegación por las correcciones y caídas del mercado

Las correcciones y caídas del mercado pueden ser inquietantes para los inversores, pero son una parte natural del ciclo de inversión. Saber cómo navegar estos períodos difíciles es crucial para mantenerse en el camino hacia la libertad financiera. En esta sección, discutiremos estrategias para manejar las correcciones y caídas del mercado con confianza:

1. Mantenga una perspectiva a largo plazo: Recuerde que invertir es un esfuerzo a largo plazo. Si bien las fluctuaciones del mercado a corto plazo pueden ser preocupantes, centrarse en sus objetivos financieros a largo plazo puede ayudarlo a mantenerse comprometido con su estrategia de inversión y evitar tomar decisiones impulsivas basadas en condiciones temporales del mercado.

2. Diversifique su cartera: Una cartera bien diversificada puede ayudar a mitigar el impacto de las correcciones y caídas del mercado. Al distribuir sus inversiones en diferentes clases de activos, sectores y regiones, puede reducir el riesgo de pérdidas significativas durante las recesiones del mercado.

3. Apéguese a su plan de inversión: las correcciones

y caídas del mercado pueden evocar emociones fuertes, lo que puede llevar a una toma de decisiones irracional. Para evitar tomar decisiones impulsivas, apéguese a su plan de inversión y mantenga su asignación de activos objetivo, incluso durante condiciones de mercado desafiantes.

4. Evite las ventas de pánico: Vender sus inversiones durante una recesión del mercado puede bloquear pérdidas y obstaculizar su capacidad de recuperación cuando el mercado se recupera. En lugar de vender en pánico, considere mantener sus inversiones existentes o incluso aprovechar la oportunidad para comprar inversiones de calidad a precios más bajos.

5. Promedio de costo en dólares: invertir regularmente una cantidad fija de dinero, independientemente de las condiciones del mercado, puede ayudarlo a navegar por las correcciones y caídas del mercado. Esta estrategia, conocida como promedio de costo en dólares, le permite comprar más acciones cuando los precios son bajos y menos acciones cuando los precios son altos, lo que podría reducir su costo general de inversión.

6. Cree un fondo de emergencia: Tener un fondo de emergencia suficiente puede ayudarlo a cubrir gastos inesperados sin tener que vender sus inversiones durante una recesión del mercado. Trate de tener

al menos 3-6 meses de gastos de manutención ahorrados en una cuenta líquida y accesible.

7. Busque asesoramiento profesional: Consulte con un asesor financiero durante las correcciones y caídas del mercado para obtener orientación sobre cómo administrar sus inversiones y mantenerse en el camino hacia la libertad financiera. Pueden proporcionar asesoramiento experto y ayudarlo a tomar decisiones informadas basadas en sus objetivos financieros y tolerancia al riesgo.

Al implementar estas estrategias, puede navegar por las correcciones y caídas del mercado con confianza y mantener su progreso hacia la libertad financiera. Recuerde que las recesiones del mercado pueden presentar valiosas oportunidades de inversión y que un enfoque disciplinado a largo plazo es clave para lograr sus objetivos financieros.

10.3 Preparación para la inversión para la jubilación

A medida que se acerca la jubilación, su estrategia de inversión debe evolucionar para reflejar sus objetivos financieros cambiantes y su tolerancia al riesgo. Prepararse para la inversión para la jubilación implica cambiar su enfoque de acumular riqueza a preservar el capital y generar ingresos sostenibles. En esta sección, discutiremos las consideraciones clave para preparar su cartera para la jubilación:

1. Reevalúe su tolerancia al riesgo: A medida que se acerca la jubilación, su tolerancia al riesgo puede disminuir, ya que tendrá menos tiempo para recuperarse de posibles pérdidas de inversión. Considere ajustar la asignación de activos de su cartera para reflejar un perfil de riesgo más conservador, con un mayor énfasis en bonos y otras inversiones de renta fija.

2. Concéntrese en la generación de ingresos: En la jubilación, su cartera de inversiones debe proporcionar un flujo constante de ingresos para cubrir sus gastos de subsistencia. Concéntrese en inversiones que generen ingresos regulares, como acciones, bonos y anualidades que pagan dividendos. Considere reasignar una parte de su cartera a estos activos generadores de ingresos.

3. Diversifique sus fuentes de ingresos: Depender de una sola fuente de ingresos en la jubilación puede ser arriesgado. Diversifique sus fuentes de ingresos invirtiendo en una combinación de acciones, bonos, bienes raíces y otros activos generadores de ingresos. Esto puede ayudar a garantizar un flujo de ingresos más estable y reducir su vulnerabilidad a las fluctuaciones del mercado.

4. Evalúe las anualidades y pensiones: Las anualidades y pensiones pueden proporcionar ingresos garantizados de por vida, lo que las convierte en opciones atractivas para la planificación de la jubilación. Evalúe los beneficios potenciales de comprar una anualidad o invertir en un plan de pensiones como parte de su estrategia de inversión para la jubilación.

5. Planifique las distribuciones mínimas requeridas (RMD): Si tiene cuentas de jubilación con ventajas fiscales, como una 401 (k) o IRA, tenga en cuenta las distribuciones mínimas requeridas (RMD) que deberá tomar a partir de los 72 años. Desarrolle un plan para retirar estos fondos e incorporarlos a su estrategia de ingresos de jubilación.

6. Mantenga un fondo de emergencia: Incluso en la jubilación, es esencial tener un fondo de emergencia

para cubrir gastos inesperados. Trate de tener al menos 6-12 meses de gastos de manutención ahorrados en una cuenta líquida y accesible.

7. Monitoree y ajuste su cartera: revise regularmente su cartera de inversiones para asegurarse de que permanezca alineada con sus objetivos de jubilación y tolerancia al riesgo. Realice los ajustes necesarios para mantener su asignación de activos objetivo y adaptarse a las condiciones cambiantes del mercado.

8. Busque asesoramiento profesional: Consulte con un asesor financiero para desarrollar un plan integral de inversión para la jubilación adaptado a sus necesidades y objetivos específicos. Pueden ayudarlo a tomar decisiones informadas sobre su cartera, asignación de activos y estrategias de ingresos para garantizar que esté en camino de una jubilación cómoda.

Al seguir estos pasos para preparar su cartera para la jubilación, puede garantizar una transición sin problemas de la acumulación de riqueza a la generación de ingresos y mantener su libertad financiera a lo largo de sus años dorados.

10.4 Mantenerse informado y adaptarse a los cambios del mercado

Los mercados financieros están en constante evolución, y mantenerse informado y adaptarse a estos cambios es crucial para mantener su libertad financiera. En esta sección, discutiremos estrategias para mantenerse actualizado sobre los desarrollos del mercado y ajustar su enfoque de inversión según sea necesario:

1. Lea regularmente las noticias financieras: Manténgase informado sobre las noticias y desarrollos del mercado leyendo publicaciones financieras de buena reputación, como The Wall Street Journal, Financial Times o Bloomberg. Seguir a expertos de la industria y comentaristas financieros en las redes sociales también puede proporcionar información valiosa sobre las tendencias del mercado y las oportunidades de inversión.

2. Asista a seminarios y seminarios web de inversión: participe en seminarios, seminarios web y otros eventos educativos para mantenerse al día sobre las estrategias de inversión y los desarrollos del mercado. Muchas instituciones financieras y organizaciones de la industria ofrecen recursos educativos gratuitos para ayudar a los inversores a mantenerse informados y tomar mejores decisiones

de inversión.

3. Conéctese con otros inversores: Unirse a clubes de inversión o foros en línea puede proporcionar oportunidades valiosas para conectarse con otros inversores y aprender de sus experiencias. Compartir conocimientos y perspectivas con personas de ideas afines puede ayudarlo a mantenerse informado y adaptarse a los cambios del mercado de manera más efectiva.

4. Controle sus inversiones: revise regularmente el rendimiento de sus inversiones para asegurarse de que permanezcan alineadas con sus objetivos financieros y tolerancia al riesgo. Esté preparado para hacer ajustes a su cartera a medida que cambien las condiciones del mercado o a medida que evolucionen sus objetivos financieros.

5. Evalúe nuevas oportunidades de inversión: Manténgase abierto a explorar nuevas oportunidades de inversión y clases de activos. A medida que cambian las condiciones del mercado, pueden surgir nuevas oportunidades de inversión que pueden ayudarlo a diversificar su cartera, generar ingresos o capitalizar las tendencias emergentes.

6. Revise y ajuste su estrategia de inversión: Revise periódicamente su estrategia de inversión

para asegurarse de que sigue siendo apropiada para sus objetivos financieros, tolerancia al riesgo y condiciones actuales del mercado. Esté preparado para ajustar su estrategia según sea necesario para adaptarse a los cambios del mercado y mantener su progreso hacia la libertad financiera.

7. Consulte con un asesor financiero: Consulte regularmente con un asesor financiero para discutir su estrategia de inversión y cualquier ajuste necesario en respuesta a los cambios del mercado. Un asesor financiero puede proporcionar información y recomendaciones valiosas basadas en su experiencia y conocimiento de los mercados.

Al mantenerse informado y adaptarse a los cambios del mercado, puede tomar mejores decisiones de inversión y garantizar que su cartera permanezca alineada con sus objetivos financieros. Adopte un enfoque proactivo para administrar sus inversiones y continúe aprendiendo a navegar por el panorama financiero en constante evolución en su viaje hacia la libertad financiera.

NOTAS:

NOTAS:

NOTAS:

Marko van Gaans

An In-Depth Case Study of Management 3.0 Practices in Action.

Wu-Wei Institute Press

Hong Kong

wuwei-inst.org

To Jurgen for helping me find my path.

"You never change things by fighting the existing reality.

To change something, build a new model that makes the existing model obsolete."

Richard Buckminster Fuller

Contents

Part III – Retrospective

List of Figures

Acknowledgements

To be honest, there are too many people to thank. From the Management 3.0 team, to all my previous workshop attendees and consultancy clients, and my beta readers whose ideas and suggestions I listened to and embraced.

I don't want to just put an extensive list of names and run the risk of forgetting someone, so I won't. **You know who you are** *and I thank you in all sincerity.*

The one exception I want to make here is for Comma Coffee, a small chain of coffeehouses in Vientiane, Laos. It has been my work with them that gave me the idea for this case study and so I'm eternally grateful to the staff and management of that company for igniting the spark of inspiration.

Foreword

For many years, I have told people stories about coffee. I shared my experience of walking for half an hour to the best coffee house in San Francisco, only to find it closed for the holidays because they forgot to update their opening hours on Google Maps. I shared my story of asking for coffee recommendations in Melbourne but then choosing to go to a Starbucks because the fancy coffee bar had no places available to sit. And I shared my story of asking for a cafe latte in Warsaw and then, to my utter horror, being served a latte macchiato because nobody had taught the barista the nuances of his trade. Without context, these stories mean nothing to anyone. But in the right place and at the right time, a good coffee story helps people to learn something important, about business, life, or leadership.

Now, from Marko van Gaans, I learned that a salary formula worked for the employees at a coffeehouse. I learned how the baristas were able to self-organize with the help of a delegation board. I also learned that customers in this coffee bar offer feedback with emoji cards and a happiness board.

Isn't it amazing how people can get creative around a few cups of brown bean juice?

It has been more than ten years since I came up with the term *Management 3.0*. Since then, I have never stopped learning how to work with teams, how to lead organizations, and how to start new businesses. It is an honor and a pleasure to see that others take Management 3.0 practices into places and environments that I had never imagined. The principles of good people management and leadership are indeed practically universal. Still, it never ceases to amaze me how creative minds can turn any mundane company with dull jobs into a great place to work.

With the case study in this book, wonderfully described by Marko, we now have a tasteful new perspective on Management 3.0 practices, and many exquisite examples to try out in your workplace.

Marko tricked me into writing this foreword by putting a tasty-looking coffee picture on the cover of his book. It worked. And so here it is. I forgive him because there's a good story in there as well.

Jurgen Appelo
Author of *Management 3.0*
and *Managing for Happiness*
Rotterdam, June 2020

P.S. I wrote this while sipping a cafe latte in one of my favorite coffee places in my hometown. Always practice what you preach.

Books by Jurgen Appelo
jurgenappelo.com

Preface

At every Management 3.0 Foundation workshop I facilitate, at one point or another, someone will ask, "Are there any case studies on this topic?" And my answer will ineffably be, "Not really."

The reason for this is that, although there's a lot of research and other material available, Management 3.0 isn't a fixed framework like Scrum or Six Sigma and so you can't just copy-paste it into your organization and religiously follow the rules.

Instead, Management 3.0 is more like an ongoing discussion on how to improve management and organizations that implement the practices tend to pick and choose the ones most suitable for them. But can you then say they are Management 3.0 organizations? Not really.

The rationale, I think, people have for wanting to read a case study is that it's hard to visualize Management 3.0 practices in action. The general feedback on workshop activities is almost always positive, but many attendees can't quite get their heads around on how to successfully implement the practices they learnt into their own organizations.

As I said, there aren't really any organizations *(yet)* that have gone full Management 3.0, but there are many that have implemented certain practices. Bosch Power Tools, for example, has used *kudo cards* and *delegation poker* to improve their corporate culture and the event management giant Eventbrite has experimented with *moving motivators*. In Italy, Agile Coach Valerio Alba has successfully introduced *delegation boards* and *celebration grids* at Vodafone.[1]

Perhaps the most comprehensive study to date is a book written by my fellow workshop facilitator Dominik Maximini, in which he describes how the German IT consulting and software development company NovaTec applied Management 3.0 practices and principles on their agile transformation journey.[2]

It's a thorough, almost 200 pages book, but NovaTec's field of operations is quite specialized and, as a result, I don't think the book can really help an inexpert reader understand the strengths of Management 3.0 practices.

This is why I decided to write my own case study. To help the general public *(you)* visualize Management 3.0 practices in action, I present to you the case of the Naked Espresso Café.

Why a coffeehouse, you may wonder. Well, there're a couple of reasons for this, but the main reason I chose a coffeehouse is because everyone can relate to it. I'm sure you've spent some time in a café, working away on your laptop, with a free refill next to you. And you've probably had your fair share of, "Why don't they just..." moments when you were questioning the way the place was run.

You can imagine what it would be like to run a café and you can imagine the frustrations an underpaid barista might have to deal with. This is why I think the story of a coffeehouse's journey towards Management 3.0 will be easier for you to visualize than let's say the abstract environment of a software company.

How to Read this Book

For the sake of simplicity, I've divided this book into three distinctive parts:

Part one, the Versioning Backstory, is a comprehensive overview of management theory throughout the ages and an introduction to complexity thinking, which is an integral part of Management 3.0. I believe this backstory is a valuable prologue to the case study that follows it but, if you feel it adds nothing new to your existing knowledge, you could skip ahead and dive straight into part two.

Part two contains the meat of this book, the Management 3.0 Case Study. I've outlined this part in line with the six organizational points of view Management 3.0 focusses on: Energize People, Develop Competence, Grow Structure, Empower Teams, Align Constraints and Improve Everything. Each of the chapters contains a bit of Management 3.0 theory, intermixed with some practical case study examples.

Part three, to conclude, is a retrospective in which I look back on the case study by means of an after-action review, an introduction to the *celebration grid* and a 'playbook' to help you implement Management 3.0 practices into your own organization.

So, three parts and some of you might only really be interested in the second one and that's fine. The other two parts, in that case, will be an incentive to dip into the book every now and then.

Disclaimer

I've done my research and collected feedback from my workshop attendees and consultancy clients. Also, one of my first clients was a coffeehouse in Laos who asked me to train their shop manager, which I did using Management 3.0 practices. But if you go to Sheung Wan in Hong Kong today, you won't find a coffeehouse called Naked Espresso nor any of their employees as introduced in this book.

Does this mean this book is just a work of fiction? No not at all, but as all my actual case study material comes from a vast variety of sources and many different fields of expertise, simply compiling them would result in a collection of random anecdotes with no clear context or structure.

This may have worked for philosophical giants like Marcus Aurelius or Nietzsche, but it doesn't suit me. I want to take my readers on a journey and have them feel a personal connection to the material.

For this reason, I felt it would be most useful if I were to piece together a fictional context and share that Management 3.0 journey with you. To me this seemed the only way in which I could create a compelling, easy to read, narrative that will help the reader *(you)* visualize the Management 3.0 practices portrayed effectively.

One last comment about the fictional employees introduced in this book. The characters might be fictional, but the ideas and opinions they express are not. They come from my own recollections of talks I had with real people but they might not be the exact words spoken at the time and are not written down to represent word-for-word transcripts. Rather, I've retold them in a way that evokes the feeling and meaning of what was said and I may have adjusted them slightly to better match the narrative of the story. But the essence of the dialogues is always accurate.

Well, there you have it. I've written a case study I would want to read myself and I hope you'll enjoy the story of the Naked Espresso Café as well and that it will inspire you to try out some Management 3.0 practices in your own organization.

Marko van Gaans
Philosopher-in-Residence
Wu-Wei Research Institute

Part I

Backstory

Why Management 3.0?

"Management of the work is a crucial activity, but this could be done with or without dedicated managers. In fact, a business can do a lot of management with almost no managers!"
~ Jurgen Appelo

Okay, first why Management 3.0, what does it mean? Well, as you might have guessed, the 3.0 refers to a semantic versioning sequence number as used in software development. It could be argued that management started with a beta release version and then gradually evolved through the 1.0, 1.5, 2.0 and so on versions and currently we find ourselves at Management version 3.0. So how did we get here?

The β-version

Once upon a time there was no management. Sure, there were nobles controlling their serfs and minions, but you wouldn't call that management, would you? Then there were also the self-employed, the subsistence farmers, tradesmen and merchants but they weren't really managed by anybody either. Basically, management as we view it today is a relatively new concept which didn't emerge until the late 19ᵗʰ century. Management thinking, however, is a lot older than this.

Arguably the first strategic management thinker would be the Chinese general, military strategist, writer and philosopher Sun Tzu (ca 544-496 BCE). Although his most famous work, *The Art of War*, mainly concerns itself with military leadership, his ideas can easily be applied to strategic business decisions as well. His approach to management is in many ways similar to what is today referred to as transformational leadership. According to Sun Tzu, effective leaders inspire their followers through leading by example. He advises the leader to, "regard your soldiers as your children and they will follow you into the deepest battles".[3] Modern-day managers following this principle would show deep concern for the careers and well-being of their subordinates, inspiring them to superior performance.

A couple of centuries later, the three great-grandfathers of Western philosophy, Socrates, Plato and Aristotle, also had something to say about management. Although they didn't talk in terms of businesses and employees, their ideas can easily be translated to modern managers' concerns of how to build productive, loyal and ethically-minded teams of employees so that their companies might flourish.

Socrates (ca 470-399 BCE), best known for his views on ethics, observed that, "those who understand how to employ others are successful directors of private and public concerns and those who do not understand will err in the management of both".[4]

Socrates' student Plato (428-348 BCE) then introduced the concept of the division of labour in book II of his seminal work *The Republic* by explaining that the inhabitants of the ideal state exchange goods and services with each other and that this exchange will be for the good of all.[5]

The last of the big three, Aristotle (384-322 BCE), provides numerous insights into the management of organizations. On the specialization of labour, he said, "Every work is better done which receives the sole and non-divided attention of the worker," and also wondered if offices should be divided according to, "the subjects with which they deal or according to the persons with which they deal."[6] To this he added his ideas about centralization versus decentralization and the delegation of authority by asking, "Should one person keep order in a market and another in some other place or should the same person be responsible everywhere?" Finally, on the topic of leadership, he remarked, "He who has never learnt to obey can never be a good commander."[7]

Further to the East, a treatise on statecraft, economic policy and military strategy, known as the *Arthaśāstra*, was written in India sometime between the 2nd century BCE and the 3rd century CE.

The manuscript, the work of several authors, deals with human motivation and dissatisfaction and the observations made in it are as modern as they are ancient, as are its prescriptions about maintaining order.[8] The book also comment on the desired traits of administrators and how to select personnel through interviews and references.

In 325 CE, at the first Council of Nicaea, the assembled bishops formulated an answer to Aristotle's question about the centralization of authority by adopting the *Credo Nicaea* in an effort to dispel some of the organizational and theological problems that early Christianity faced.[9] In modern organizational terms, the Catholic church leaders perceived the need to institutionalize the organization by specifying policies, procedures, doctrine and authority. With the Bishop of Rome now as the Supreme Pontiff and leader of the Catholic Church, the European Christian nations assumed the world's wealth was static (*cf.* Mercantilism[*]) and consequently, attempted to accumulate the largest possible share of that wealth by maximizing their exports and limiting their imports via tariffs. It's safe to say that management thinking then entered a status quo.[10]

But then the inventions of the power loom and the steam engine kicked off the Industrial

---

[*] An economic theory and practice common in Europe from the 16th to the 18th century which was the economic counterpart of political absolutism.

Revolution and things changed forever. When the revolution was in full swing, the once semi-independent rural workforce moved en masse towards metropolitan areas to become employees, working for a 'boss' in urban factories; the professional manager, albeit a crude one, had been born. Let's call this the beta version of Management.

In the early days of this beta version a boss was just that, the chief at the top of a pyramid giving orders, making rule-of-thumb decisions and ultimately accountable for the results of his (yes, they were all men) employees. However, faced with the Luddite Rebellion* in the early 19th century, these early managers had to find more effective ways to motivate and control their workers. What they came up with is what we now refer to as the 'carrot and stick' method of management. Positive inducements being the carrot and negative sanctions being the stick emerged. In an effort to build a new factory ethos, this became the prevailing method of providing motivation and maintaining discipline.

Throughout the 19th century, numerous beta managers added ideas to development of the theory. Welsh textile manufacturer Robert Owen, for example, experimented with moral suasion rather than corporal punishment on his workers. This led

---

* The 1779 uprising of English textile workers in Manchester against the introduction of machinery which threatened their skilled craft. It was the first of many Luddite riots to take place.

to his main contribution to management thinking: the *Silent Monitor*. The way this worked was that he placed a block of wood in each of his machines with its four sides coloured either black, blue, yellow or white in ascending order of quality. At the end of the workday, performance was noted by a supervisor who would turn the block to display the appropriate colour. This way his employees could keep track of each other's performance and see if anyone were slacking off.[11] This invention was definitely a precursor of contemporary management's public posting of sales and production data to instil departmental pride or encourage competition.

In 1855, Scottish-American railroad superintendent, Daniel McCallum, designed an illustrative diagram of the New York and Erie Railway, which is considered to be the first modern organization chart.[12]

The steel magnate Andrew Carnegie, another Scottish-American, then added to the managerial toolbox that a manager should always watch costs before anything else and also was the first entrepreneur to use vertical integration as a business strategy.[13]

As the 19th century drew to a close, the beta release of management had steadily developed into its first fully mature iteration.

Management 1.0

French management theorist Henri Fayol (1841–1925) and American mechanical engineer Frederick Winslow Taylor (1856–1915) are generally seen as the founding fathers of what we now refer to as Management 1.0 because they both realized the importance of management for industrial progress and, as a result, endeavoured to develop a rational and systematic basis for management. Fayol's *Principles of Management* and Taylor's *Principles of Scientific Management* are mutually complementary although they differ on several aspects.

Fayolism

Fayol, a bourgeois in post-revolutionary France, believed that controlling workers in order to achieve greater productivity should be prioritized over all other executive considerations. His key idea was that by focusing on managerial practices it should be possible to minimize misunderstandings and increase efficiency in organizations. In his main work, *General and Industrial Management,* he outlines an agenda whereby, under an accepted theory of management, every citizen is exposed and taught some form of management education and allowed to exercise management abilities first at school and later in the workplace.[14]

During the early 20th century, Fayol developed his, now famous, *14 Principles of Management*

7

theory to help managers manage their organizations more effectively. They are as follows:[15]

1. **Division of Work** – When employees are specialized, output can increase because they become increasingly skilled and efficient.

2. **Authority** – Managers must have the authority to give orders, but they must also keep in mind that with this authority comes responsibility.

3. **Discipline** – Discipline must be upheld in organizations, but methods for doing so might vary.

4. **Unity of Command** – Employees should have only one direct supervisor to report to.

5. **Unity of Direction** – Teams with the same objective should be working under the direction of one manager, using one plan. This will ensure that action is properly coordinated.

6. **Subordination of Individual to General Interests** – The interests of one employee should not be allowed to become more important than those of the group. This includes managers.

7. **Remuneration** – Employee satisfaction depends on fair remuneration for everyone. This includes financial and non-financial compensation.

8. **Centralization** – This principle refers to how close employees are to the decision-making process. It is important to aim for an appropriate balance.

9. **Scalar Chain** – Employees should be aware of where they stand in the organization's hierarchy, or chain of command.

10. **Order** – The workplace facilities must be clean, tidy and safe for employees. Everything should have its place.

11. **Equity** – Managers should be fair to staff at all times, both maintaining discipline as necessary and acting with kindness where appropriate.

12. **Stability of Tenure of Personnel** – Managers should strive to minimize employee turnover. Personnel planning should be a priority.

13. **Initiative** – Employees should be given the necessary level of freedom to create and carry out plans.

14. **Esprit de Corps** – Organizations should strive to promote team spirit and unity.

Within his theory, Fayol outlined five practical elements of management that depict the kinds of behaviours managers should engage in so that the goals and objectives of the organization are effectively met. These five managerial elements are:

Planning ~ Organizing ~ Commanding Coordinating ~ Controlling.[16]

Planning here means that managers should create a plan of action for the future, determine the stages of the plan and decide in advance on what to do, how to do it, when to do it and who should do it. This maps the path from where the organization currently is to where it wants to be. The planning element also involves establishing long and short-term goals and arranging them in a logical order.

Once a plan of action has been designed, managers need to provide everything necessary to carry it out. They need to organize raw materials, tools, capital and human resources. In addition to this, they need to identify responsibilities, group them into departments or divisions and specify the organizational relationships.

Employees will perform at their best if they are given concrete instructions with respect to the work they need to do. Successful managers have integrity, communicate clearly and base their decisions on regular audits. They are capable of motivating the team and encouraging employees to take initiative.

When all activities are harmonized, the organization will function better. Therefore, coordinating aims at stimulating motivation and discipline within teams. This requires clear communication and good leadership. Only through positive employee behaviour management can the intended objectives be achieved.

The final element of management involves comparing the activities of the employees to the plan of action, aimed to keeping the manager in control. This is a four-step process in which the manager first establishes performance standards based on organizational objectives. Next the actual performances will be measured and then compared to the established performance standards. Finally, corrective or preventive measures will be taken as required.

Henri Fayol's theory of management has been a significant influence on modern management theory and can be viewed as one of the main pillars of Management 1.0. His practical list of 14 principles and five functions of management helped early 20th century managers learn how to organize and interact with their employees in a more productive way.

Although the principles aren't widely used today, they can still offer guidance for modern managers. Also, although many of these principles are now considered to be common sense, at the time they were revolutionary concepts for organizational management. But then came along a whole new set of ideas.

Scientific Management

Whereas Henri Fayol was mostly concerned with the improvement of overall administration, his American counterpart Frederick Taylor's main focus was on improving the overall productivity of an organization. Recognized as one of the first management consultants, Taylor was an intellectual leader of the early 20th century Efficiency Movement and his ideas were highly influential from the 1890s to 1920s. In 1911, he published a book titled *The Principles of Scientific Management* in which he proposed that by optimizing and simplifying work, productivity would increase. He also put forth the idea that workers and managers needed to cooperate with one another, which was quite different from the way work was typically done in businesses beforehand.[17]

First of all, he argued that the widespread rule-of-thumb work methods of early managers were to be replaced with the scientific study of an employee's tasks. Even a small production activity like loading iron sheets into box cars could be scientifically planned, he claimed, as this would help saving time as well as human energy. Decisions should, therefore, be based on scientific enquiry with cause and effect relationships and not on intuitive trial and error methods. Rather than making educated guesses, managers should constantly be experimenting systematically to develop new techniques with the aim to make the work simpler, easier and quicker.

He further emphasized that there should be complete harmony between the workers and the management since if there is any conflict between the two, it won't be beneficial for either of them. Instead of being left to their own devices, employees should be scientifically selected, trained and provided with detailed instruction and supervision. Moreover, an atmosphere should be created in the organization in which labour (the major factor of production) and management consider each other indispensable. Taylor often referred to a 'mental revolution' which involved a change in the attitude of workers and management towards one another. Both should realize the importance of each other and work with full cooperation. Management and the workers should aim to increase the profits of the organization together.[18]

He then expanded on his theory of harmony by further stressing the importance of mutual cooperation between workers and the management. Workers should be treated as an integral part of an organization and all important decisions should be taken after due consultation with them. On their part, workers should resist going on strikes or making unnecessary demands from management. Foreshadowing the evolution of management, Taylor also argued that workers should be considered as part of management and should be allowed to take part in the decision-making processes.

Finally, he figured that the work should be equally divided between managers and workers, so that the managers could apply scientific management principles to planning the work and the workers could effectively perform the tasks they were set. More importantly, employees should be assigned work best suitable to their physical, mental and intellectual capabilities and should be provided with training if necessary. Efficient employees produce more to earn more and this ultimately helps to attain efficiency and prosperity for both the organization and its employees.

To prove his theories, Taylor conducted a number of experiments he referred to as time and motion studies. One of the most famous of these involved shovels. Taylor noticed that workers used the same shovel for all materials and deemed this to be ineffective. After careful observation and study, he determined that the most effective load a worker could handle was about ten kilos and designed shovels that for each material would scoop up exactly that amount. The predictable result was a fourfold increase in production. Prior to Taylor's scientific experiment, workers had used their own shuffles and rarely used one optimized for the job.[19]

Fordism

Often considered a spin-off of Taylor's Scientific Management is Fordism. Aptly named after the US automobile pioneer Henry Ford (1863-1947), Fordism is a manufacturing philosophy that aims to improve productivity by standardizing the output, through the use of conveyor belt assembly lines, and breaking the work into small unskilled tasks. Whereas Taylor's Scientific Management seeks machine and worker efficiency, Fordism seeks to combine them as one unit, and emphasizes minimization of costs instead of maximization of profit.[20]

At an organizational level, the Management 1.0 model was pure centralized command-and-control implementing formal hierarchies of positions and rules. The CEOs at the top with senior managers reporting to them, and middle managers reporting to them, and so on. All these management layers followed pre-defined rules and policies. The employees at the bottom of the pyramid were disempowered. They just did as they were told, executing specific highly broken-down tasks and often unaware of what their exact input in the bigger picture was. Basically, workers were mere cogs in a grandiose machine.

Management 1.0 was suited well to the large industrial factories of the 19th and early 20th centuries in which employees were mainly concerned with turning raw materials into more complex stuff and which didn't require a whole lot of 'knowledge work'. But this was about to change.

Management 2.0

The 1960s saw the rise of Management 2.0 which was the result of two important industrial and economic changes. The first major change was the increasing automation of factories. As a consequence, industry needed fewer manual labourers and more technically specialized staff who were able to operate and maintain the more complex machinery now in use. Besides this a large service industry emerged with a need for skilled knowledge workers rather than unskilled manual labourers.

Theory Y

The preeminent management theory behind what is here referred to as Management 2.0, was developed by Professor Douglas McGregor of MIT's

Sloan School of Management. McGregor's main argument was that, "people aren't dumb automatons to be bossed around, threatened and harassed; they are beautiful precious souls who need to be nurtured and grown".[21] He coined the Scientific Management pioneered by Taylor as Theory X in which, he claimed, employees are characterized as people who don't want to work and don't care for the organizations they work for. In contrast, he proposed a Theory Y in which employees do want to work and do care about the organizations they work for if and only if they are treated with respect and kindness. Building relationships with employees and developing their abilities and knowledge should be the primary role of managers.[22]

In the hippie turmoil of the sixties and seventies, McGregor's ideas caught on. Instead of replaceable cogs in a machine, employees were now seen as beautiful snowflakes who should be nurtured and given hugs if they felt bad. It was also the time which saw the rise of HR departments, career plans and professional development programmes.

In terms of evolution, Management 2.0 was definitely a step in the right direction, but it still relied too much on hierarchies, centralized command-control and specialization. Another technique lingering on from the Management 1.0 era was the carrot and stick method of management, albeit now with more emphasis on the carrot, through the promises of bonuses and promotions, than on the stick.

A further development in the Management 2.0 era was the implementation of project management or the practice of delegating work to a team which then had to achieve specific goals and meet clear-cut success criteria within a specified timeframe. Although this did somewhat address the delegation of command and control, there was a problem with it. Project management is great for the kind of work where the expected outcomes are well-known upfront but it's not that effective for situations with a lot of uncertainty around their value proposition, i.e. most of the work in the late 20th century.

Lean: The Toyota Production System

Also in the 1960s, the seeds were sown for what we now refer to as Lean Manufacturing when two Japanese industrial engineers at the Toyota Motor Company, Taiichi Ohno and Eiji Toyoda, developed the socio-technical Toyota Production System (TPS). The main objectives of the TPS are to avoid overburden *(muri)*, inconsistency *(mura)* and to eliminate waste *(muda)*.[23] To successfully achieve these objectives, the TPS adheres to the underlying principles of continuous improvement *(kaizen)* and respect for people.[24]

By the 1990s, Lean Manufacturing, as the TPS had become known as, got company from Agile Development theory. Whereas Lean has its roots in industrial manufacturing and mainly focusses on the process and quality, Agile is based around software development and concentrates on scope and value.[25] This basically means that Agile is about building one new thing for only one time, while Lean is about building the same thing over and over again. In manufacturing, variation and rework are bad, but in development they are good. Most agile development methods break product development work into small increments that minimize the amount of up-front planning and design and are completed in short time frames or iterations. At the end of an iteration a working product is demonstrated to stakeholders. This minimizes overall risk and allows the product to adapt to changes quickly.[26]

The 1990s also saw a revival of a practice called System Thinking with the publication of the book *The Fifth Discipline* by Peter Senge, a researcher at MIT.[27] Systems Thinking moves away from traditional analysis methods, in which systems are studied as separately broken-down elements, by focusing on the way that a system's constituent parts interrelate and how systems work over time and within the context of larger systems.[28]

Building on this theory, which was developed in the 1950s at MIT's Sloan School of Management, Senge's book applied Systems Thinking to organizational theory and knowledge management. Systems Thinking has been of great influence on the work of later management theorists, especially Jurgen Appelo and Dave Snowden and thus foreshadowed the leap to Management 3.0 in the years to come.

Management 3.0

Since the 1990s, both the Lean and Agile management theories have made big strides. Many organizations are realizing the limitations of McGregor's Theory Y and some of the more daring ones have moved towards the model of Servant Leadership. In this model, championed by many in the Agile movement, the main role of managers is to help their subordinates do their work, not to boss them around.[29] To a certain extent, this has been the defacto role of managers in Lean Manufacturing in Japan since the 1960s where workers define and improve their work and managers help them by providing the tools and support needed to get the work done.

However, at a structural level not much has changed. This is because traditional organizational structures and bureaucratic models are rigid and thus resistant to change. As a result, Lean hasn't really adopted Servant Leadership properly. Even the Japanese organizations that led the way still have giant static bureaucratic structures with set roles and hierarchies.

In the fast and volatile corporate environments of today this just won't do. Every day, the market demands quicker answers to its problems and needs. If the decision-making capability remains centralized and specialized, organizations will quickly lose momentum. In traditional 1.0 and 2.0 organizations, decision processes often are too slow because of the centralized and specialized intelligence of decision which creates a series of bottlenecks in the process of decision making. And this is where Management 3.0 enters the stage.

As a theory, Management 3.0 is the brainchild of Dutch management theorist Jurgen Appelo who is the author of the aptly named book *Management 3.0* in which he describes the role of managers in agile organizations,[30] and *Managing for Happiness* in which he offers practical ideas to engage workers and improve the work culture.[31]

The philosophy of Management 3.0 builds on Management 2.0 by decentralizing the intelligence of decision or viewing management as a group responsibility. This doesn't mean that anyone can just do whatever they want. It means allowing the right people to make the right decisions at the right time so that they will produce results in the fastest possible manner. As long as the right constraints are in place and managers manage the system, not the people, decentralized control will create maximum value for any organization. Not too bad, right? But, of course... this is easier said than done.

The first step in adopting the Management 3.0 mindset is to make sure everybody is aware of your effort, be open and transparent about it. Basically everybody today has grown up in a world based on hierarchical structures and so most employees don't realize that they should also be responsible for management, that it is a joint performance.

However, it is important to stress that Management 3.0 is not aiming to get rid of management, nor is it a remodelled form of communism. Rather, Management 3.0 is a commonsensical way to transform the role of the manager into an enabler for the collective intelligence of decision. The 3.0 manager fosters an environment set up to help individuals and teams make better informed decisions.

Any manager can adopt the 3.0 mindset regardless of their organizations' structure. As long as managers aim to manage the system and not the people, their staff will take care of themselves and consequently, Management 3.0 means better management with viewer managers.

One other caveat I'd like to make here is that Management 3.0 is not yet another framework. It's not the next Lean, Scrum, Six Sigma, Holocracy or whatever. It is not a set of rules for you to follow. Instead it is more about attitude then structure. It is a set of practices to help employees help their managers manage an organization. The tools and practices of Management 3.0 will be easier to implement in more flexible and organically structured organizations, but it is possible to put the concepts into practice in even the stiffest hierarchical organizations.

Why Even Bother?

By now, you're probably wondering why this shift to Management 3.0 would even be necessary, aren't most organizations today regarded as being 2.0 and aren't they doing just fine? And yes this is true but, as I mentioned earlier, Management 3.0 isn't a framework to implement in an organization. It's an evolutionary next step in the ongoing development of management. You could just hobble along and ignore new developments but then you risk falling behind like once dominant organizations like Kodak, Blockbuster and Nokia did when they resisted adapting to new ideas on time.[32]

Moreover, managers with a 1.0 or 2.0 mindset tend to fall back on predictable systems and certainty and by doing so they risk making some potentially catastrophic mistakes.

Before looking at these potential mistakes, let's first have a look at an example of how the world today has become more complex. You probably remember the Central Perk coffeehouse from the 1990s sitcom *Friends*.

When the show launched in 1994, a simpler time, a coffeehouse was a place where you'd meet your friends and your choice of coffee in most cases was either a black coffee or a coffee with milk and sugar, maybe an espresso or cappuccino in fancier places.

Nowadays, however, the coffeehouse has become a place for work where people mostly interact with their devices and the regular cup of Joe has turned into dozens of different options, ranging from an *Americano* and *Flat White* to *Eiskaffee* and *Kopi Tubruk*. And then there's the variety of different brewing methods, from a standard drip to the French press or a cold brew, you can even opt for the 'cowboy' method recently popularized by the foodie community.

Now, of course this isn't really an example of complexity, but I do think it paints a clear picture of how, on a daily basis, we have to deal with far more information than ever before. Some even claim that a weekday copy of the *New York Times* contains more information than an average 17th-century person would encounter in a lifetime.[33] Although this famous factoid should be taken with a grain of salt, it is certainly true that we are bombarded by immense amounts of information (and misinformation) in comparison to even the recent past and that processing all this information is complex.

Our build-in defence for dealing with these increasingly complex situations is to rely on what we know and already understand, i.e. to simplify the complexity. As mentioned previously, 1.0 and 2.0 managers want certainty and predictability but trying to force this within a complex situation might lead to four serious managerial errors.

1.0 & 2.0 Erroneous Thinking

1. The first and most common mistake is the tendency to prioritize numbers over people. Now of course numbers are important for business. Not knowing your profit margins, cash flow or returns on investments would spell disaster. However, not everything can be neatly expressed in numbers. For example, only focusing on the appraisal rankings of your employees to gauge their performance is a mistake. The complexity of human behaviour cannot possibly be expressed in numbers alone.

2. Another situation in which the 1.0 or 2.0 mindset errs is the tendency to design systems instead of growing them. Examples of this are creating an office layout and not wanting to adjust it when needed or forming teams and not reorganizing them if necessary. Another example is that too often once a plan has been made, that's it, we should all stick to the plan. An unforgivable mistake! When I was in the army, we were always told that, yes, we should plan all our actions but only with the realization that those plans would become obsolete the moment we executed them. The only reason to make those plans in the first place was that you need a starting point to deviate from.

3. The third mistake 1.0 and 2.0 managers make is that they rely too much on indirect over direct communication. Of course, written company

policies and a steady flow of progress reports are necessary but relying on these alone is not enough. As human beings we are social animals and require face-to-face communication. Vocal cues and body language convey messages that the written word can't and texts are much more open to interpretation, so people might come to conclusions that the writer never intended (this despite the efforts of overly enthusiastic emoji designers).

4. The fourth and possibly most disastrous mistake is that the sum of the previous three will lead to everybody pointing at each other as the cause of problems. When there's no real communication, an inflexible work environment and an overreliance on numbers, it becomes easy for people to hide behind this and avoid taking any kind of responsibility.

In and of itself numbers, systems and paper communication aren't necessarily a problem but, when approached with a Management 1.0 or 2.0 mindset, they might lead to the four mistakes we just covered, which in turn might cause the managers to fall victim to the micromanagement trap.

The *(avoidable)* Micromanagement Trap

Micromanagement is exactly what it sounds like; a manager trying to personally control and monitor everything in a team, situation, or place. While this is sometimes useful (e.g. in small-scale projects), micromanagement usually results in the manager losing track of the bigger picture and, worse than this, it is universally loathed by those being managed. Micromanagers watch every move their staff make and demand progress reports way more often than necessary. They chastise individual team members for the slightest mistake they make or for carrying out a task differently to how they would have done it themselves. Always watching their teams up-close, picking apart every mistake made or deviating from the task set without clear communication, micromanagers are guaranteed to demotivate their staff.

So, the question is how to avoid micromanagement? In line with Management 3.0 thinking, I would argue that the answer to this question lies in accepting that the traditional structures of organizations, which once provided the craved certainty and predictability, are long gone. Instead organizations today have evolved into complex adaptive systems, i.e. environments that are always adapting to ever changing circumstances.

Complex Adaptive Systems

A Complex Adaptive System (CAS) is any system in which a group of semi-autonomous agents, who interact in interdependent ways, produce system-wide patterns which in turn influence the behaviour of the agents. Some examples of complex adaptive systems are countries, gardens, cities, immune systems and beehives.[34] Huh(?), I can hear you think, let's look at the Swindon Magic Roundabout in the United Kingdom as an example (figure 1)[35].

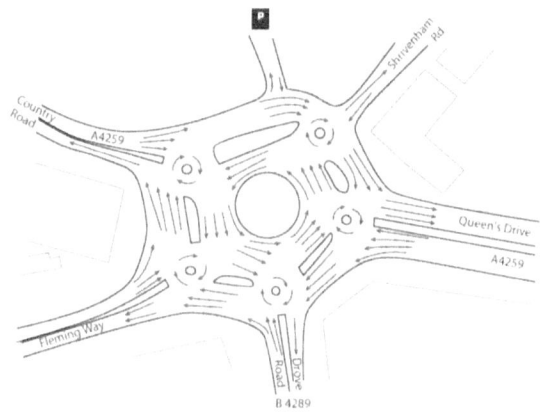

Figure 1: Swindon's Magic Roundabout, UK.

Constructed in 1972, Swindon's Magic Roundabout is a ring junction consisting of five mini roundabouts arranged in a circle around a sixth central circle. The outer circle carries traffic in a clockwise direction, like regular roundabouts (in places where traffic drives on the left-hand side of the road), and less proficient users may choose to only use the outer circle. The inner circle carries traffic in an anticlockwise direction, and more proficient users may choose to use the alternative paths.[36]

On this roundabout you find agents, which would be the vehicles. These agents all interact and are free to make their own choices. For example, drivers can decide to stay 'safe' and remain in the more traditional outside ring or they may make use of the more adventurous small inner roundabouts and at some point even find themselves going against traffic. Whatever choices they make, over time some interactions will happen more frequently than others and so these will generate system-wide patterns of behaviour that come to characterize the system as a whole. Subsequently those patterns will then reinforce the behaviour of the individual agents, which brings us full circle.[37]

CAS Behaviour & Structure

Another way to look at complex adaptive systems is to study their behaviour and structure. Simply put, we can argue that there are three basic behaviours of a complex adaptive system and two possible structures (figure 2).[38] [39]

The first behavioural domain is the ordered or the known.* These are the elements of a complex adaptive system that we know and understand.

---

* I've based my explanation of CAS behaviour and structure on David Snowden's *Cynefin* framework and Jurgen Appelo's criticism of Snowden's work.

The ordered domain represents stable situations in which the relationship between causes and effects is usually crystal clear.

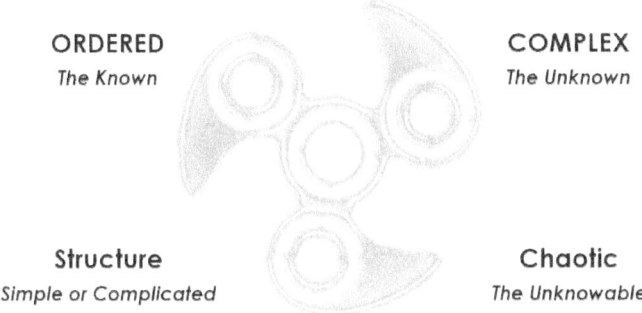

ORDERED
The Known

COMPLEX
The Unknown

Structure
Simple or Complicated

Chaotic
The Unknowable

Figure 2: CAS Behaviour and Structure

Next, we have the complex or unknown domain. In this domain what causes what effect is unclear and can only be deducted in retrospect. It's unknown but through deductive analysis and experimentation it can become knowable. Some examples of complex domains are battlefields, markets and corporate cultures, each of which requires a take-it-apart-and-see-how-it-works approach to fully understand them.

Finally, there's the chaotic or unknowable domain. In this domain events are too confusing for knowledge-based responses. Chaos needs instinctive action in an effort to turn it into a complex situation. Examples of the chaotic domain are terrorist attacks or financial market crashes.

Those are the three different domains of a complex adaptive system and each of these can be structured in one of two ways: they're going to be either simple or complicated. For example, rolling dice. Rolling a die is in the chaotic domain, you can't scientifically predict the outcome (unless they are loaded, of course), but it's also simple because there are only six possible outcomes. You either roll a 1, 2, 3, 4, 5 or 6, there are no other options. A market crash, on the other hand, is also in the chaotic domain and infinitely more complex, there will be innumerable interrelated causes of the crash. That brings us to the question, how do you deal with complexity?

Understanding Complexity

As the Chinese sage Confucius once remarked, "we need to be aware of what we know and don't know."[40] I would argue that there are four distinct kinds of knowledge:

There are things you know you know;

things you know you don't know;

things you don't know you don't know, and;

things you didn't know you knew.

The first two are straight forward. From the moment we are born, we embark on a life-long learning journey and all the things we actively learn along this path become the things we know we know. By their nature, this means that we continuously encounter unknowns, the things we then realize we know we don't know. The challenge is to tackle what we don't know and transform it into something we know.

The third form of knowledge, the things we don't know we don't know, harks back to former US Secretary of Defence Donald Rumsfeld who said, "There are the unknown unknowns; the ones we don't know we don't know." [41] A simple example, you can't know that Ouagadougou is the capital of Burkina-Faso if you don't know there's a country called Burkina-Faso.

Finally, the fourth form of knowledge, which I find the most fascinating, the idea that there are things we don't know we know. It was introduced by the Slovenian psychoanalytic philosopher Slavoj Žižek in reaction to Rumsfeld's comments. Žižek's rather dark interpretation of the 'unknown knowns' is that they are those things we do know but intentionally refuse to acknowledge.[42] In other words, the facts we turn a blind eye to because they represent an inconvenient truth.

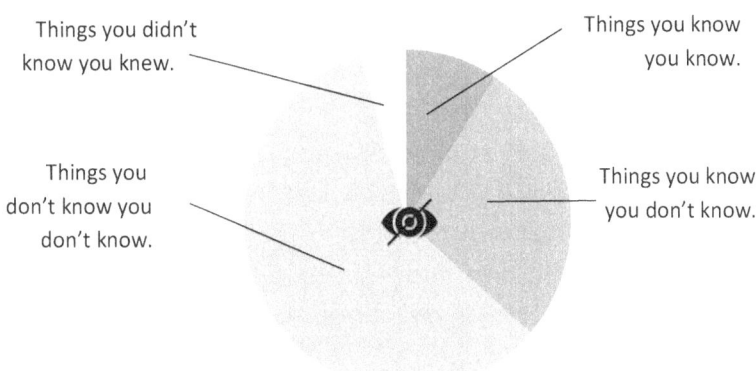

Figure 3: The four types of knowledge

Visualizing Complexity

Once we've aligned our knowledge, a good way to deal with complexity would be to visualize where we find ourselves. Let's map things out in a CAS decision-making landscape (figure 4).

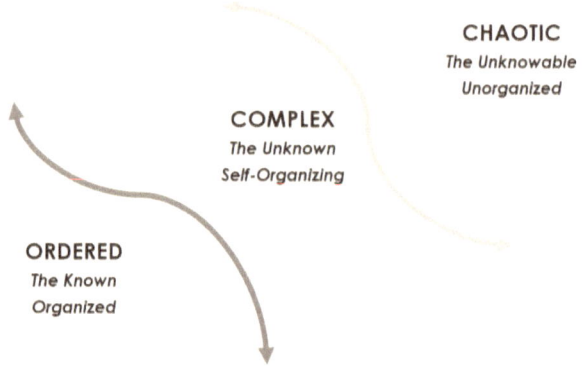

CHAOTIC
The Unknowable
Unorganized

COMPLEX
The Unknown
Self-Organizing

ORDERED
The Known
Organized

Figure 4: CAS Decision-Making Landscape

There are three areas in the CAS decision-making landscape. In the safe zone on the left we find the ordered domain; the things we know and are organized in ways we understand. On the other side of the spectrum we find the chaotic danger-zone, just unknowable, unorganized chaos. And in between the two there's the domain of the complex. The issues in this domain may be unknown and unorganized, but they are knowable and as such can be organized, often from the bottom-up through self-organization. So how does this help me deal with complexity, I can hear you think. Well, let's have a look at them one by one.

The ordered domain is the most straightforward one. When managers are confronted with simple issues in the ordered domain, all they need to do, after they recognize they're dealing with an ordered issue, is to categorize it and act. A complicated issue in this domain requires a bit more action. Before categorizing it, the issue might need some analysis by experts before rational action is taken. But overall, the ordered domain is the one where a manager's training and experience pay their dues.

In the complex domain traditional management approaches are rather ineffective. To deal with complex issues, managers need to continuously probe and experiment to correctly identify the issues before taking appropriate action; it's a great opportunity to unleash creativity and innovation from the ground up and create new models of operation. It is also the domain of self-organization where teams learn from their mistakes.

Then the chaotic, the unknowable domain which any rational manager dreads. Issues that come up in this domain display high levels of uncertainty and disagreement, often disintegrating in total anarchy. To deal with these issues managers need to rely on their intuition. There's no time to analyze or rationalize, action needs to be taken. Once the situation is somewhat under control, managers need to probe and experiment until they can make some rational sense of the issue at hand. Once they have a better grip, they'll need to adjust the actions earlier taken.

To summarize, the ordered domain requires rational decision making, knowledge and skills. In the complex domain you'd focus on creative decision making and experimentation. And finally, in the chaotic domain you'll have to rely on instinct and making gut-feeling decisions. Rational, creative and intuitive, sounds simple enough. But, of course, this is easier said than done.

Dealing with Complexity

To help you out a bit, Management 3.0 proposes eight guidelines to deal with complex adaptive systems. Unfortunately, there aren't any natural laws we can use to deal with complexity, the best we can do is to adhere to these guidelines:

1. **Address complexity with complexity.** This may sound a bit confusing, but it isn't really. A mistake often made when dealing with complex issues is trying to categorize them as you would an ordered one. Instead of doing this, it will be more effective if you try to break the complex issue down into smaller parts and accept the issue at hand is a complex one. As the saying goes, "admitting you have a problem is the first step in fixing the problem."[43]

2. **Use a diversity of perspectives.** Different people view things in different ways. So, by acknowledging that there are other ideas than your own, whether they're right or wrong, a

diversity of perspectives will give you a clearer picture of the complex problem.[44]

3. **Assume subjectivity and co-evolution.** This also may sound a bit abstract but, like with addressing complexity with complexity, if you break down the problem into smaller parts and begin your inquiry with the parts you understand, then they in turn will clarify the ones you don't yet understand.

4. **Steal and tweak.** Very straightforward, I think. There's no need to keep reinventing the wheel. Instead search for already existing solutions to similar issues and adjust them to your own situation.

5. **Expect dependence on context.** Another straightforward piece of advice. Everything is dependent on context. So, what worked once might not work again and what worked for others might not work for you, or at least not in the same manner.[45]

6. **Anticipate, explore and adapt.** This is about being proactive and willing to experiment as complex adaptive systems by their nature involve experimentation.[46]

7. **Shorten the feedback cycle.** Although it might be more interesting trying to work out something as a whole, with complex systems it's much more effective to run lots of small experiments

and learn step-by-step how the complex issue really works. So, iterate faster.[47]

8. **Keep your options open.** Actually, some advice for anything you do in general. Plan but accept that plans stop working once you execute them. So, just go with the flow and allow yourself to be surprised.

A Little Brain Teaser

Besides following the previous eight guidelines, another way to train yourself to deal with complexity is to play around with brain teasers. Give this one a try. What does the formula below really say?

$$\sqrt{-1} \ \ 2^3 \ \ \Sigma \ \ \pi$$

and it was delicious.

Answer:

Well, it's obviously a sentence clause as there is the conjunction *and*. So let's decipher, the square root of -1 is impossible, in mathematics notated as 'i.' Two to the third power is eight, which sounds like *ate*. The sigma symbol in accounting is used to sum things up, and sum sounds like *some*. Finally, the pi symbol sounds like *pie*. So, the full formula reads: "I ate some pie and it was delicious."

Part II

Case Study

Prelude

*"If you do not change direction, you
may end up where you are heading."*
~ Laozi

After the historic overview of Management 1.0, 2.0
and 3.0, an explanation of the complex-adaptive reality we live in these days and some guidelines on
how to deal with this complexity, it's time for the
meat of this book: a Management 3.0 Case Study.

Although the tools and practices of Management
3.0 can be applied to any organization, people often
have a hard time conceptualizing the actual practical change these tools and practices can bring to
their own businesses. For this reason, I've decided
to help you visualize Management 3.0 in action
with an in-depth case study of the:

Naked Espresso Digital Nomad Café.

Picture a somewhat ramshackle two-story Chinese
shophouse on a corner of a lively side street just off
Des Voeux Road in Central Hong Kong's trendy
Sheung Wan area. In this shophouse, five friends,
Melvin, Maria, Sean, Kim and Joyce — who all
wished to escape the pressure of the 60 to 70-hour

workweek an average Hong Kong office worker has to endure — created their own Central Perk and christened it Naked Espresso Digital Nomad Café.

It is a home away from home (or actually an office away from the office), catering to the fast-growing community of digital nomads, trendy young IT-savvy hipsters who earn their living online working on their laptops and using laid-back coffeehouses as their basecamps.

The café has two main streams of income. On the ground floor there is the traditional coffee shop which serves a variety of coffees and other beverages as well as light healthy lunches and hearty snacks. Then, on the first floor, there is a coworking space where people can rent hot desks by the hour or a dedicated desk on a monthly basis. With the desks comes a shared space where the nomads can print or copy documents and there are mailbox lockers for those who use the shop as their virtual address. The floor is completed with a fully outfitted meeting room for eight which can also be rented by the hour. Finally, on the mezzanine between the ground and first floor, there is the office of the five owners who keep a watchful eye on the shop floor below.

The café didn't start out embracing the Management 3.0 philosophy. The five friends didn't really know what they were doing but, as they entered the market at the right time, they managed to make it work; financially that is. So, what drove them to Management 3.0? Let's be a fly on the wall and find out.

Flumppf, the *South China Morning Post* hit the floor after Maria hurled it across the mezzanine office above the main floor of the coffeehouse in central Hong Kong.

"I don't understand it Sean, I just don't get it!" she roared, pulling her hair back in a vexed motion, plaiting it in an effort to calm herself down. "We've only been running this place for a couple of months yet all we seem to do is train new staff. Why do they keep leaving?"

"I don't know," said Sean, looking up from his laptop, "maybe this wasn't such a good idea after all."

With a deep sigh Maria pulled up a chair and sat down. But it had been a good idea, she thought. She recalled the American sitcom *Friends* and how she and her friends had liked to act out its different scenes when they were in middle school, even though they didn't quite understand the lives they were copying. She always chose to be Phoebe, the quirky one.

When she'd graduated with a master's in Maritime Law from the City University of Hong Kong in 2014, she'd been lucky to find a job almost immediately at Jardines, one of the original legendary Hong Kong trading houses. But had it been lucky, really? Life in the city was fast-paced and expensive, and as an office worker, especially a junior one, you were expected to work long hours, 60-70 hour workweeks easily being the standard rather than an exception.

"You remember Sean," she said glancing at her friend who had once again turned his attention to his laptop, "this was our dream, you know... you, me, Melvin, Kim, Joyce. Our own Central Perk right here in Central."

"Yes, of course I remember," said Sean, "but maybe it was just a dream. Maybe we're not right for this. After all, none of us has a background in hospi—"

"But that's why we hire staff!" Maria interjected. "They're the ones with the hospitality background."

It all had seemed such a simple idea when the five of them had met that breezy Sunday afternoon on Lamma Island a couple of years ago. They were all tired of their jobs — not even 25 and basically burnt-out already — so they made a pact, they would leave the corporate rat race and start their own Central Perk.

It seemed a natural choice. At that time all over Hong Kong these so-called coworking spaces were popping up but none of them had the *je ne sais quoi* of *Friends'* Central Perk; there just had to be space for a place like it. Moreover, there was a fast-growing community of digital nomads, flocks of trendy hipsters independently making money online with laptops and a coffeehouse as their place of work. As for the five of them, Melvin, who was related to one of the Four Big families*, had the cash. Kim was a trained CPA, Joyce was good for her creative input, Maria had the legal and business

---

* The **Four Big families** refers to the four Chinese-Hong Kong business families who rose to prominence during the British colonial rule in Hong Kong. They are Li, Ho, Hui and Lo.

acumen and Sean was all IT savvy. What a team to start a Digital Nomad Café!

Over the next couple of months they put their ideas into motion. They found the perfect spot, a two-storey shophouse for a surprisingly reasonable annual rent, in the trendy Sheung Wan neighbourhood in Central. Then, one by one, they quit their jobs, ready for the adventure to begin. Sadly, this was also when the trouble began.

It wasn't the business itself that caused problems. They had been right, there was a market for a *Friends*-like café. Open from 10:00 to 19:00, the café always had a healthy number of patrons and at lunchtimes it could even be called crowded. No, there was another issue. As neither Maria, Sean, Melvin, Kim or Joyce had any background in the hospitality business, there had been one flaw in their otherwise flawless plan.

Digital Nomads thrive on a steady input of caffeine, a healthy snack or meal every now and then and, most importantly, a fast Internet connection and impeccable IT support. They had the IT covered, Sean was an absolute magician when it came to computers and a fast Internet connection was just a matter of picking the right provider and making sure you paid the bills on time. For food and beverages, on the other hand, they had to rely on hired help. This had seemed a non-issue. After all, how hard could it be to find some kitchen staff and waiters in a city of seven million people? And indeed, finding staff wasn't the problem. No, retaining them was.

"Why do they keep quitting after just a couple of weeks?" Melvin asked with a sigh, putting down his mug of *flat white* just a bit too hard, attracting the attention of the other four team members in the mezzanine.

"I don't know," Maria replied in a voice almost trying not to be heard. She had taken on the role of Front of House manager a few weeks ago after the group had decided that their original plan of rotating as floor managers didn't work out as they had hoped. But this week another two employees had given their notice and one had simply disappeared.

"Well, I don't know either," Melvin said, adjusting his glasses, "It can't be the money, we pay them more than most of our competitors."

"Actually, that could be it," Joyce added to the conversation. "We may be paying them well, but that's just not good enough anymore these days."

"What do you mean?" Melvin and Kim asked in unison.

"Well, I read this book... uhm ... it's called *Managing for Happiness* which is all about how extrinsic motivators like salaries and bonuses aren't quite enough anymore to retain your staff these days."

"So what then? People don't work for money anymore? Do they need hugs or something?" Melvin spewed his questions with irritation in his voice.

"No, of course not," Joyce replied, "but the book introduces a number of 'tools' which it claims should motivate people beyond their paycheck. I think we should have a look at it and see if there's anything which we could use."

"I think that's a good idea," said Sean who had been kind of taking a backseat so far. "We're obviously doing something wrong, so I can't hurt."

"Agreed!" Maria exclaimed as Kim and Joyce also nodded their heads in agreement. "What about you Melvin?"

"Fine," Melvin responded, "Anything to get this mess fixed."

To the Rescue!

And that's when I got a call, and Naked Espresso's journey on the path to Management 3.0 began.

Could I help them out? They had decided to implement Management 3.0 tools and practices in the café but weren't quite sure how they should do it. After all, none of the Management 3.0 books had been written with a coffeehouse in mind.

I decided that the most straightforward way to successfully implement Management 3.0 in their business was to do so step-by-step by bringing into play the six change management points of view as I cover them in my Management 3.0 Foundation workshops:

Energize People   **Empower Teams**
Develop Competence   **Align Constraints**
Grow Structure   **Improve Everything***

---

* The actual order in which these topics are presented may differ among Management 3.0 workshop facilitators, but this is the sequence I prefer.

Change Management Perspectives

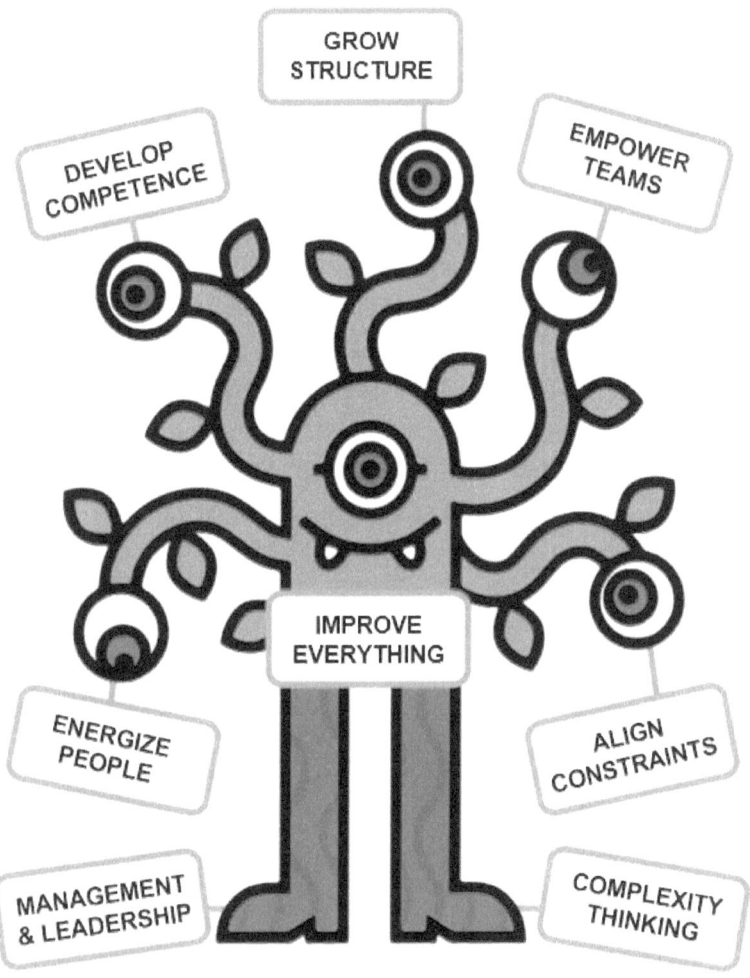

Figure 5: Marti the Management Monster © Management 3.0

1

Energize people

"If the only reason people are coming in and doing anything in your office is because you're giving them a paycheck, I'm not sure you have the most productive workplace there."
~ Daniel H. Pink

Without a doubt, people are the most important element of any business and so managers must do all they can to keep their people active, creative, and motivated. But motivating staff is probably also one of the most difficult tasks a manager has to deal with. What really motivates someone? One of the main issues here is that what is motivational for one may be a complete turn-off for another. Also, the driving force for someone at the managerial level isn't necessarily the same as that which entices the people on the work floor.

Basically, as a manager you simply won't be able to motivate everybody in the same way. However, you can definitely create the conditions which will maximize the likelihood of your staff being motivated in their work. The key here is to keep in mind that you should always aim to manage the system, not the people.

A crucial first step in managing the system is acknowledging that there are two main forces that motivate all of us, our intrinsic and extrinsic motivators. In his book *Management 3.0*, Jurgen Appelo defines intrinsic motivation as, "people's innate desire to do well, and their eagerness for self-control and self-direction in accomplishing objectives."[48] Intrinsic motivators are those factors with which you motivate yourself from the inside out whereas extrinsic motivators are those that come from outside yourself, e.g. your paycheck.

Extrinsic Motivators

Although nowadays, as they found out at Naked Espresso the hard way, money alone isn't enough to motivate staff anymore, fact is that people first and foremost drag themselves to work every day because they get paid. Therefore, I'd first like to draw your attention to two Management 3.0 practices regarding extrinsic motivation: the *salary formula* and *merit money*.

Salary Formula

Let's face it, most of us, if not all, work for money and throughout our working lives we expect to see a steady increase in remuneration and responsibilities. We'd like to climb the career ladder. This traditionally meant you'd start somewhere at the bottom as a Junior-Assistant of 'something or another', fresh out of school, and then steadily make your way up through the corporate hierarchy to hopefully become a Senior-Deputy-Vice-President of 'this or that' by the time you're ready for retirement. But how many Senior-Deputy-Vice-Presidents does an organization really need?

Point in case is a scene in the 1987 movie *Wall Street* in which the villain Gordon Gecko concludes that a company he's about to acquire has 33 Vice-Presidents, none of whom seem to add much actual value to the business. He accuses them of bringing the company on the brink of bankruptcy and unequivocally states, "Our paper company lost $110 million last year and I'll bet that half of that was spent in all the paperwork going back and forth between all these Vice-Presidents."[49]

Unavoidably, extensive career planning and increased pressure to keep everybody happy, will cause the layers within any organizational hierarchy to grow exponentially and along with this often comes a nonsensical inflation of job titles. Do you know what a Director of First Impressions does? * And this is exactly why Management 3.0 aims for management as a group responsibility with better management but fewer managers. But how do you keep staff motivated (i.e. energized) if you don't offer any promotions?

The answer lies in creating a transparent salary formula with a tiered competence structure.

---

* A *Director of First Impressions* is a *Receptionist!*

What does this mean? First, let me show you what a transparent salary formula is and why it's important.

It's 'funny' how, through the Internet and social media, our lives have become completely transparent and privacy seems to be an antiquated idea from the past. Yet, at the same time, in corporate culture there remains a final social taboo: asking your colleagues about their salary; it's none of our business. Why? Is it because most salaries are as a matter of fact rather unfair? Yes, I do think so, let me explain.

Years ago, I worked as an Operations Officer for a small airline. The operations department never sleeps and so we worked irregular hours in shifts, making sure the department could operate seven days a week and 24 hours per day. To compensate us for these irregular hours, we were given a bonus on top of our salary, or so we were told. Then, by chance, I found out that the staff at the planning department, who work Monday to Friday from nine to five, were paid exactly the same as us, the numbers were just specified differently on their payslips. No wonder the company favoured a lack of transparency.

Not knowing who makes how much and why often breeds discontent. A good salary formula, on the other hand, enhances transparency and allows employees to understand their full earning potential, what they need to do to achieve it and empowers them to define their career paths. It's a strong extrinsic motivator but also motivates staff intrinsically as we will see later in the section on intrinsic motivation.

To see a transparent salary formula in action, let's have a look at the one we created for the Naked Espresso Café.

An Ox-Rider Looking for a Horse*

Originally Naked Espresso was organized hierarchically with all the salary secrecy that goes with it. It is a picture we are all familiar with, the CEO on top of the organization chart which then spreads out to a whole range of different positions with different pay scales. The thinking behind this was that a hierarchy would allow staff to grow within the organization, but it wasn't working. After some initial discussion, it was decided to adopt a flat hierarchy with self-organizing teams (see next chapter) and the following basic salary formula was created for their staff:

(Base x Competence) + Loyalty Bonus + Inflation Correction = Salary

The first, and biggest, component of anyone's monthly income is their base salary. To calculate this, management created clearly outlined roles (i.e. not fixed positions) for the Front and Back of

---

* This Cantonese idiom 騎牛搵馬 *(ke ngau wan maa)* which is often used in reference to employment, i.e. working in one job while on the lookout for a better one.

House as well as administrative support and management staff. Next, they researched the average pay for similar roles throughout the industry and formulated a minimum base salary for each of them.

This minimum base salary is then multiplied by an individual employee's competence level, resulting in the actual base salary. This is how a transparent salary formula becomes the key to being able to provide a career plan and occasional promotions without creating a hierarchy.

At Naked Espresso, they now use four tiers of competence levels:

greenhorn, proficient, well-versed and crackerjack.

At what tier staff members will start will depend on their qualifications and experience when hired. Once employed, staff can progress through the tiers by means of in-house and external training, as well as the on-the-job experience they build up.

A *greenhorn* is someone completely new to the business, inapt and inexperienced. Not someone you'd necessarily like to have on your staff, but everybody needs to start somewhere. Naked Espresso makes room for greenhorns from a social responsibility perspective, but also because they feel a blank slate can be trained more easily. When it comes to the salary formula, greenhorns see their minimum base salary multiplied by one, i.e. no increase.

This changes for *proficient* staff. Those who are hired as proficient will see their base multiplied by 1.25. If, for example, the minimum base salary for Front of House staff is HK$ 9,500 per month, then their actual base salary will be HK$ 11,875. Requirements for the kind of schooling and previous experience to be considered proficient are clearly laid out in the café's role descriptions.

Well-versed staff members are similar to proficient staff, but with more relevant qualifications and experience to justify a higher base salary. The monthly minimum base salary of well-versed members of staff is multiplied by 1,5 so, if we keep the previous example in mind, their actual base salary will amount to HK$ 14,250.

Finally, the *crackerjacks*. These are staff members who are qualified and experienced enough to be able to train, coach and advise the other members of staff and will do so in addition to their respective regular roles in the organization. To reward them for their efforts, the base salary of a crackerjack is multiplied by two.

As the teams at Naked Espresso are self-organized and the team members have roles rather than positions, supervisors or middle-managers are not required. However, because of the different competence levels, employees are able to grow in their roles, assume more responsibilities and get 'promoted' financially. But you definitely won't find a Director of First Impressions at the Naked Espresso Café.

To complete the salary formula, a loyalty bonus and inflation correction are added. The loyalty bonus is a pay raise of 2.5% for each year an employee has served at the café. Because this raise doesn't take into account inflation, salaries are also corrected for this.

Let's now complete the picture by looking at the completed salary formulas for Ryan, a shiny new 20-year-old greenhorn at Naked Espresso and Zoë, a 19-year-old proficient barista who's been at the café for two years. Both of them are employed full-time.

Being new on the job, Ryan's minimum base and actual base salary are the same, HK$ 9,500 per month. He's not eligible for a loyalty bonus yet, but he does get the inflation correction on top of his base. The current inflation in Hong Kong is 2.4%, so an extra HK$ 228 is added, bringing his total pay to HK$ 9,728 per month.

Zoë's minimum base salary is also HK$ 9,500 but this is multiplied by 1.25 making her actual base salary HK$ 11,875 per month. With a 5% loyalty bonus for her two years of service, her income increases to HK$ 12,468.75 per month. To this is finally added HK$ 285 for inflation correction, bringing her total income to HK$ 12,753.75 per month.

Even though there's a HK$ 3,025.75 gap between the salaries of Ryan and Zoë, management can easily explain why this gap exists and justify it. In general, people tend to be not that bothered by others getting paid more than themselves as long as they understand why and feel it's justified. If Ryan wants to make more, he can find out what he should do and what trainings to participate in to qualify himself as proficient. The same goes for Zoë or any other staff member at the café who would like to move up the line financially.

I asked Ryan about his opinion and this is what he had to say:

[Ryan Kwok Bou-gwan]: *"O jui,* our Salary Formula, what I think about that? Well, at first I thought it was a bit *ma-ma-dei,* but now I think it's actually quite good. Sure, the others make more than I do, even though we do the same work, but it's okay.

"For example, I do work as a barista sometimes, but only for basic orders as I don't have any real training other than on the job by Natalie, she's a crackerjack. But there are often opportunities for training. Sometimes Natalie conducts one but other times we can sign up for some training outside of the café to get certified.

"I also know exactly which certificates I need to move up from greenhorn to proficient, so it's really just up to me to get promoted, not up to some manager to like me or not.

"To be honest, I used to be a bit of an ox-rider always looking for a horse, but here I feel like the ox is good enough so to speak."

Merit Money

Besides salaries or wages, many organizations also provide some kind of bonus as an incentive to their employees. Great! That should motivate people, right? In and of itself yes it would. However, as the financial crisis of 2007-08 made painfully clear, bonuses or other financial incentives without proper regulation can cause a whole lot of trouble.

Management 3.0, therefore, proposes a bonus system with better controls. But first, a name change. In the same way that the Ministries of War were renamed Ministries of Defence after World War II, and propaganda is now public relations, we renamed our bonus system *merit money* to remove the bad connotation caused by greedy bankers.

There are dozens of ways a merit money system might be devised and we'll look at the example of Naked Espresso soon. But to avoid the slippery slope to a free-for-all money grab it's essential to put some rules in place. Management 3.0 has come up with the following six:[50]

> Don't promise rewards in advance;
>
> Keep anticipated rewards small;
>
> Reward continuously, not just once;
>
> Reward publicly, not privately;
>
> Reward behaviours, not outcomes;
>
> Let peers reward each other.

Let me explain how each of them should be applied. The first rule, *to not promise rewards in advance* is also the most important one. The main issue with most bonus systems which led to the crash of 2007 was that they were mostly annual bonuses. Because of this people came to expect a (huge) bonus at a specified time regardless of this bonus would be justified. The bonus wasn't a bonus anymore, it had become part of the salary, a bit like how in the US a part of the wages in the service industry is reliant on tips. By not setting fixed pay-outs of the merit money, you'll avoid your staff becoming reliant on their bonuses and make sure the bonus is just that, a reward for good performance.

The rules *to keep rewards small* and *to reward continuously*, go hand-in-hand with the first one. By providing one annual bonus pay-out, expectations and in-head spending will grow incrementally. So, instead of one lump sum at the end of the year, it would be better to pay-out smaller bonuses at unannounced intervals throughout the year. Not only will this diminish expectations and reliance, but it will also reinstate the feeling of having earned a bonus within your staff.

The fourth rule, *to reward publicly*, is a bit more controversial. Most people don't enjoy being praised or rewarded in public; it makes them feel uncomfortable. However, this rule doesn't mean putting the spotlight on someone and making them the centre of attention. What it means is that bonuses should be transparent. Like with the salary formula, it should be crystal clear how much everyone gets and what they did to deserve it. As mentioned before, not knowing who gets how much and why often breeds discontent.

Number five, to *reward behaviours, not outcomes*, can be a bit tricky depending on your line of business as in most industries bonuses are by definition outcome-based. Most salespeople, for example, will receive their bonus based on the number of sales they make. But as I'm sure you can imagine, this might easily create a culture in which the sales department will do anything to make a sale, regardless of the ethical consequences. It would, therefore, be better to base the bonus on the kind of customer a salesperson brings in or the expected commercial lifespan of that customer.

Finally, rule six *to let peers reward each other*. This is probably the most interesting and unusual one. Traditionally management decides the value of the bonuses. We propose to take this out of the hands of management (remember management is a group responsibility) and involve everybody. How? Let me show you this by means of the merit money scheme we put in place at the Naked Espresso Café.

A Night at the Races

Unlike in some countries, where service workers are paid artificially low salaries so that they need to heavily rely on tips (thus breaking all the rules laid out above), this is not the case in Hong Kong and so gratuity = merit money. The question is, how do we apply those six rules to it?

Like most restaurants and cafés in Hong Kong, Naked Espresso adds a ten percent service charge to a customer's bill. Before adopting Management 3.0 practices, the amount collected this way was simply equally divided over the Front and Back of House staff once a month. Fair in a way (and covering rules two and three), but not quite fair enough to encourage staff to work harder and provide outstanding service.

After some observation and a lot of discussion we came up with the following scheme. At the beginning of every month, each member of staff, from the freshest greenhorn to the CEO, gets a hundred *kudos points*. Throughout the month (until a couple of days before payday), staff can award their kudos points to any other staff member who they believe deserves it.

There are no rules other than that they should have awarded all their points by the end of the month. It could be to a colleague who helped them out, maybe covered part of their shift or any other imaginable reason. Of course, they can't award the points to themselves, otherwise the monthly results wouldn't be very surprising.

To reward their points, staff use an app developed in-house which requires them to enter the person they reward points to and give a reason why. This can be seen by all and so provides full transparency.

In lieu of a person, they can also award points to either the Front of House, Back of House or Mezzanine (management/admin). At the end of the month the points awarded to these departments will be equally divided over their respective team members.

Okay, let's visualize this by putting some numbers on it. For simplicity, we'll assume that the café collected HK$ 10,000 in service charges for the month and look at Zhifeng, one of the kitchen staff, to see how his merit money is calculated.

At the end of the month we are looking at in this example, Zhifeng has been awarded a total of 88 kudos points by his colleagues and the Back of House department he's part of received another 109 points.

With HK$ 10,000 service charges collected and a total of 16 staff at the café, this means that 1 kudos point is equal to HK$ 6.25 (10.000 ÷ 16 ÷ 100).

As Zhifeng was awarded 88 points, he will receive HK$ 475 as his gratuity. To this is then also added another HK$ 170.31 from the Back of House department (109 points x HK$ 6.25 ÷ 4 team members). So, Zhifeng's total merit money for this month will be HK$ 645.31.

As you can see, by using the kudos points this merit money scheme already covers rules two, three, four, five and six. But how about the first rule, arguably the most important. Well, they have a night at the races.

Every last Wednesday night of the month, the whole team meets up at the Happy Valley Racecourse. Together they pick a winner for one of the races. If their horse wins, they'll get their bonus and if it doesn't, they don't (rule one). They don't lose the bonus though. Instead it will roll over to the next month, making next month's race even more exciting.

One night I joined the Naked Espresso crew at the races and asked Zhifeng and Carmen, both Back of House staff, about their experience. (Full disclosure, *Green Luck*, the horse they had placed their bet on had just won the race!)

"Woo-hoo!" Flushed faces and twinkling eyes, it's obviously been a great night.

[Carmen Lo Yin-faa]: "Did you see that? It was all hacked up at first, but then *Green Luck* won by a neck!"

[Zhifeng Wu Zeon-gwan]: "Yeah, *Quadruple Double* was the dead favourite but somehow we felt we should bet on *Green Luck*, how lucky are we?"

[Carmen]: "You know, I've been working in cafés for quite some time, but I can't think of any place where getting tips is so exciting as at our shop. Every month we have this fun night out, you know, great food, drinks the lot. Even if we don't win, it's still a fun night out and if we do win... Well, wow I got 137 kudos points this month and then there's the rollover of the past two months. I'm gonna buy me a pair of swishy heels and some bling!"

[Zhifeng]: "I agree, at most places the Back of House hardly get to share in the tips. But here we're kind of in charge of our own share. If you do well to others, they'll reward you kudos points and your share goes up. Like this month, I got 117 points!"

Intrinsic Motivators

With the extrinsic motivators covered, it's now time to look at the intrinsic motivators at the Naked Espresso Café. As I mentioned earlier, although money is important, most people don't only want to work for a paycheck anymore. As motivational speaker Simon Sinek aptly put it, "We want to work in a place with purpose, to make an impact, and we want to have free food and bean bags."[51]

Unfortunately, you can't simply force your staff to feel motivated and engaged with their work. But you can create the conditions that maximize the probability that they will feel this way (no matter how hard this may seem for some jobs). The challenge is that you need to work out what makes them tick, to know who cares about what and what puts them off. But how do you do that?

Personal Maps

"How well do you really know your staff?" This was the first question I put to the five owner-managers and chef assembled in the mezzanine at the first of many meetings during which we would aim to improve the café's staff retention and motivation. The question educed a somewhat defensive response.

"We have their CVs," Melvin said with a jitter in his voice. "And we always check references," Maria added, not missing a beat.

Although it's true that you'll learn some things about your employees from their CVs, the picture won't be complete. CVs focus on skills, not personality traits and attitudes. And as most successful leaders will confirm, you should hire for attitude and train for skills.

Moreover, to be able to work together effectively, people need to understand each other. And to understand each other, they need to know each other. The same goes for managers. To effectively manage your staff, you need to understand them and to do that, you need to know them beyond their CVs. What are their wants and needs? And especially, what puts them off?

In my days as an army instructor, way back in the 1990s, we would often be 'in the field' and spot a colonel or general wandering around, seemingly lost. These senior officers were trying to practice a management style commonly referred to as 'management by walking around', all the rage at the time.[52] This idea of being where your workers are had originated in Japan and rapidly made its way into business colleges and even military academies all over the globe.

Although the concept of *genchi genbutsu*, to go and see, sounded great in theory, a problem was that it often felt too contrived to the staff whereas most senior managers were just too uncomfortable with making blue-collar chit chat. And if they did manage to strike up a conversation, it would probably stay in the safe-zone of weather, sports and nonspecific work-related issues. Not quite the topics to get to know each other. But then what should you talk about?

This is where *personal maps* come in, another tool from the book *Managing for Happiness*. It is based on the visual brainstorming technique of mind mapping.[53] The key idea is that when you start creating personal maps about your colleagues — it's not an idea limited only to managers — you'll quickly find out how little you actually know about them. Who are they? What's their backstory? And what do they want? Now you know what to talk about.

It might seem a bit creepy and intrusive to ask people personal questions about themselves, but you'll be surprised about the appreciation most people will have for questions asked with genuine interest. After all, don't we all expose our inner thoughts, successes and failures on social media all the time in the hope of a like or retweet?

But then again, in Asia, the sociological concept of 'face' comes into play.* To counter this, I suggested a slightly adjusted approach to the personal maps activity.

---

* The Asian concept of 'face' refers to a cultural understanding of respect, honour and social standing. Certain actions may cause somebody to 'lose face' while others may 'give face'.

"The last time I cried…"

Rather than the management team creating personal maps about their staff to find out what questions to ask them, I suggested they should have a little team building session. Instead of categories with factual information attached to a person's name as the traditional approach to personal maps suggests, I asked all the staff members (yes, that includes management) to think of five anecdotal stories about events in their lives that made them into who they are today.

Next, I gave them a blank sheet of A3 paper and asked them to write their full name in the middle and encircle it. Then they were to write cryptical prompts of the stories they had thought of on the paper and connect them to their name.

We then hung the maps on the walls of the meeting room and did a walk-around. I picked the first prompt I wanted to know more about and asked the team member in question to tell the story. She then told her story and picked the next prompt, and so on. The whole thing turned into an engaging session during which everybody happily opened up and shared their stories. I feel that this was mostly because they were given the time to pick their stories and so knew what they were supposed to talk about, minimizing the risk of 'losing face'. Another interesting result was that the stories told gave rise to many questions from other members of staff and, as I mentioned before, most people appreciate

questions asked with genuine interest and cheer-
fully share more about themselves.

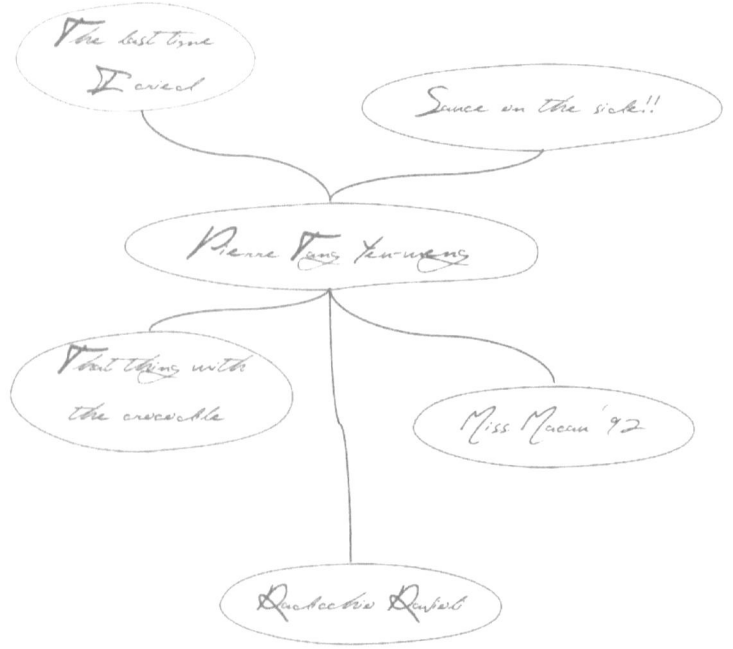

Figure 6: Personal Map © Pierre Tang Yeu-weng

Without revealing any details, the most interesting
case was when iron-fisted Chef Pierre shared a
moving story enticed by the prompt, "The last time
I cried" (figure 6). It was fascinating to see how this
(perceived) nightmare of the kitchen visibly gained
respect in the eyes of his crew.

All in all, this little personal maps teambuilding
session proved to be a valuable tool for all involved
to get to know, and thus understand, each other
much better.

CHAMPFROGS Moving Motivators

To dive even deeper into the abyss of staff motivation, Jurgen Appelo created the tool of CHAMP-FROGS moving motivators, for which he studied the work of Daniel Pink, Steven Reiss and many others, and identified ten factors of motivation that might positively or negatively influence people at work.[54] Just so you know, the word CHAMPFROGS doesn't actually mean anything, it's just a silly acronym to help you remember the ten motivators. This being said, it's a great tool to help identify what truly motivates and engages your staff, so let's have a look at what those letters stand for.

C = Curiosity – Having plenty of things to investigate or think about.

H= Honour – A feeling of pride that your personal values are reflected in your work.

A = Acceptance – Receiving approval for who you are and what you do from others.

M= Mastery – When your work challenges your competence but within your abilities.

P = Power – Being able to influence what is going on around you.

F = Freedom – Being independent of others with your own work and responsibilities.

R = Relatedness – Having good relationships with your colleagues and/or customers.

O = Order – Having enough rules and policies in place to create a stable work environment.

G = Goal – Finding that your (self-identified) purpose in life is reflected in the work you do.

S = Status – The position you hold and the recognition you receive from others.

In the book *Managing for Happiness,* Appelo also outlines the *moving motivators* 'game' which you can play with your staff to visualize what makes them tick.[55] Playing the game is pretty straightforward. Every player receives a deck of cards in which each card represents one of the ten factors of motivation. After reading through the cards, they then individually arrange them to rank from least to most important.

There's no right or wrong order in this exercise, everyone will have their own priorities. Experience has taught me that, despite its simplicity, this game can be an eye-opening experience for people to learn about each other. But the question remaining, of course, is what can a manager do with this information? Let me show you how Naked Espresso managed to get some mileage out of the game.

More than just a bleep on the radar

After being introduced to the moving motivators, Maria and Pierre, who manage the Front and Back of House, weren't immediately enthusiastic. "It's not clear," they argued. "What is the difference between power and freedom and what self-identified purpose in life does working in a coffeehouse have?" Valid points, but the mistake they made was that they got stuck on semantics.

The words that make up the CHAMPFROGS acronym are just that: words. Any word in the English language will have many different meanings, depending on the context in which it is being used. Facilitators of a moving motivators game should explain their own definitions of the cards' words before allowing participants to put them in order of importance.

Once this caveat was made, Maria and Pierre got started with the activity. They gathered their teams and had them lay out their cards. As expected (by me anyway), the results surprised them. Whereas they both had curiosity and order at the top of their lines, most of the staff prioritized freedom and acceptance. Maria was also a bit disappointed to learn that only Natalie and Zoë ranked mastery reasonably high on their lines, a trait she thought was essential for baristas.

Surprises and disappointment aside, moving motivators is an effective reflection tool. The main take-away is to never assume others are like yourself. Everybody is wired differently, a valuable lesson for both managers and their staff. To visualize the data gathered, Maria and Pierre created some attractive looking radar charts (figures 7 and 8).

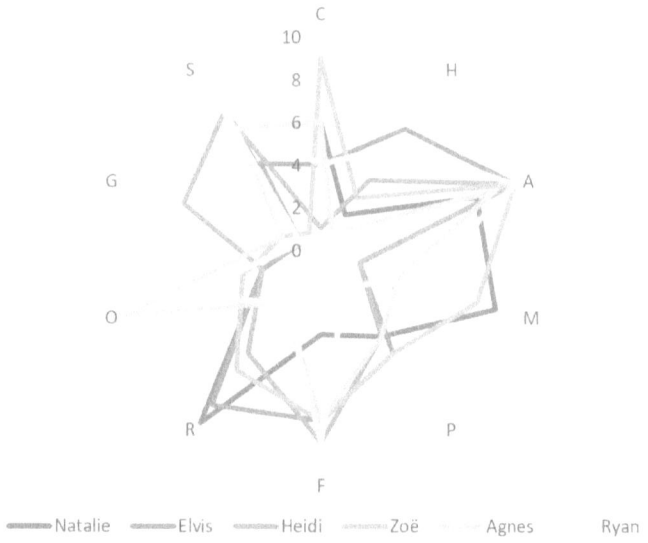

Figure 7: CHAMPFROGS Radar Chart of Front of House Team

The real power of CHAMPFROGS doesn't lie in pretty graphs, of course. Once you know what motivates and demotivates who, you can use this information to your *and their* advantage. Let's look at the line of Elvis, a well-versed staff member on the Front of House team, to see what I mean.

As you can see on the Front of House team chart (figure 7), Elvis' two most important motivators are acceptance and relatedness whereas mastery and curiosity rank at the bottom of his line. On a quiet afternoon, Maria sat down with a steaming mug of coffee and had a brainstorm session to figure out what she should do with this information.

Acceptance was an easy one. Elvis (as do most of his colleagues) feels more motivated if he can be

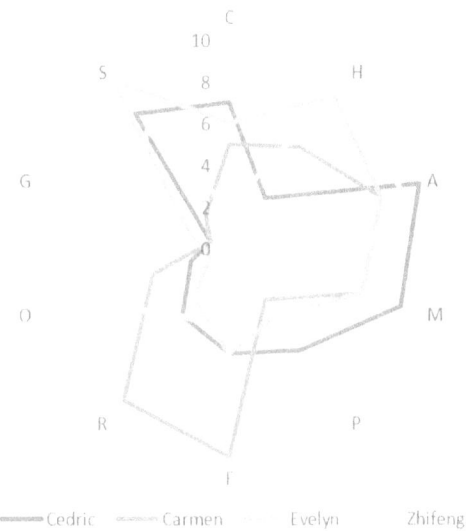

Figure 8: CHAMPFROGS Radar Chart of Back of House Team

himself, so she figured she should let him. For example, she decided she could be less strict on dress codes and general appearance as most of the customers couldn't care less what the staff looked like anyway.

Concerning relatedness, as he is well-versed, Elvis will probably spend most of his time behind the coffee machines composing fancy brews and adorning them with his latte art. A lonely place when it comes to interacting with others. One way to deal with this, Maria figured, was to let him serve his creations to the customers and allow him to strike up conversations with them. As for socially interacting with colleagues, Maria felt that the monthly trips to Happy Valley (see merit money) more than covered that. Small and easy to implement gestures that should make Elvis feel happier at work.

Trickier were the things that demotivate him. Again like most of his colleagues, Elvis doesn't care much about mastery. This means that he doesn't enjoy stepping out of his comfort zone. The best way to deal with this, and his lack of curiosity, Maria thought, was to not rethink the drinks menu too often and to make in-house training voluntary rather than mandatory.

Sometime after the changes had been implemented, I asked Elvis, how he felt about them.

[Elvis Chiu Yam-tu]: *"Oh zeoi,* is that's what's been going on! I was wondering why everybody suddenly stopped complaining about my goatee. Well, if it's because of that card game, I'm glad we played it. I do feel better at work right now and I do enjoy talking with customers more."

As you can see, with just some small tweaks and gestures it's very possible to create a work environment in which an individual staff member will feel more comfortable and thus more motivated. Of course, you can't tweak everything and you can't make everybody a hundred percent happy. But, as Maria and Pierre found out, the effort alone creates a lot of goodwill among the staff.

An Experiment with Emoji Cards

A final thing Maria decided to do to improve the intrinsic motivation of the service staff, was to run an experiment with customer feedback. In the hospitality industry, praise is normally expressed in tips. However, in Hong Kong tips have mostly been replaced by service charges, so how can a customer individually praise an employee who's done an outstanding job without double tipping?

I'll discuss the experiment Maria decided to run in more detail in the next chapter, but the short version is that when customers receive their bill, they also get three emoji cards. One with a delighted face, an ambivalent one and a displeased one, together with some space for the customer to express their feelings in a percentage (figure 9).

Figure 9: Customer Feedback Emoji Cards

Customers can then pick the card that best expresses how they feel about the service in the café, add a percentage expressing their happiness score and stick it on a pinboard next to the entrance. Throughout the day, the board functions both as a happiness index for customers' experience and a feedback tool for the staff and management.

Now that we had the basics covered, fair pay and a motivating work environment, as an ongoing project that is, it was time to get the teams up to speed. In the next chapter, we will take a look at the next point of view for Management 3.0, which is to develop competence.

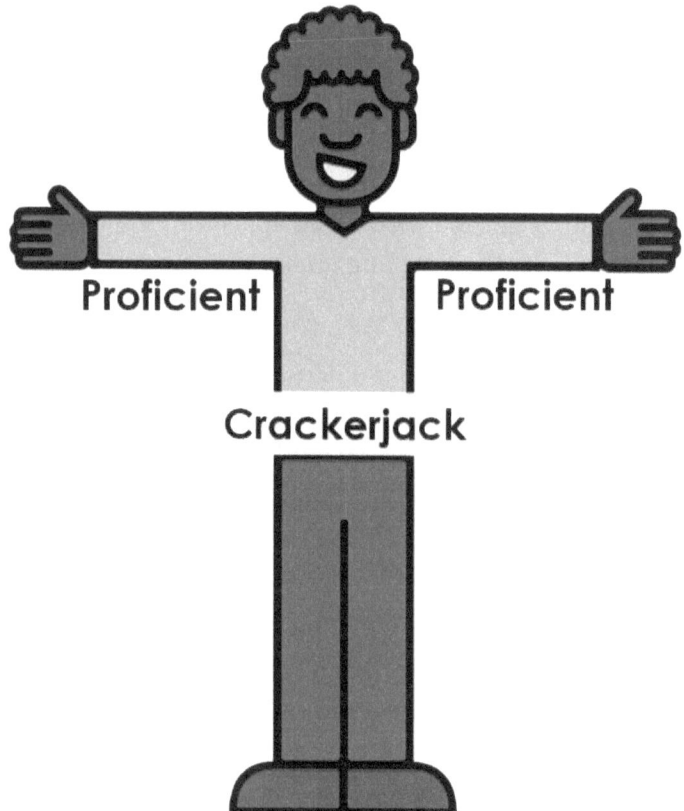

Figure 10: T-Shaped Employee © Management 3.0

2

Develop Competence

> *"I fear not the man who has practised
> 10,000 kicks once, but I fear the man who has
> practised one kick 10,000 times."*
> ~ Bruce Lee

As any sports coach will tell you, "a team is only as strong as its weakest player" and the same is true for teams at the workplace.[56] For this reason, an organizational environment of continuous learning is essential to create strong, valuable and competent teams. But what makes a team competent?

The first thing we can identify is that any team will consist of a combination of the following team members, *novices* (those who are inexperienced), *skilled members* (those who have experience) and *experts* (those who are willing and able to teach the inexperienced).

At the Naked Espresso Café, these team members are known as *greenhorns, proficients* and *crackerjacks*. Ideally, skilled and expert team members will be what is commonly referred to as *T-shaped employees*, i.e. specialized in one area but also experienced in other relevant areas (figure 10).

Team Competence Building Blocks

If we break the structure of teams down into components that influence team competence it can be argued that there are four main building blocks: *individual competence, helping each other, team communications* and, perhaps most important of all, the *creative tension* within a team (figure 11). By improving these four elements, a team is bound to become more competent.

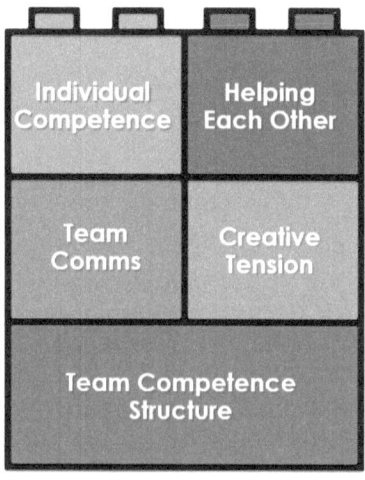

Figure 11: Competence Building Blocks © Management 3.0

The strength or competence of a team can only be as good as the sum of its members, so the main focus of team improvement should be on individual competence development. There are a number of factors which should be taken into consideration for this, but first and foremost managers should lead by example. It's basic human nature to copy observed behaviours so, if managers commit themselves visibly to professional development, they will sow the seeds for a learning culture and continuous learning environment within an organization. We'll further explore other options to develop individual competence in a bit.

The second block is all about team members *helping each other*. As with developing individual competences, the key here is for managers to lead by example. Further options would be to organize internal mentoring programmes or run short workshops. An alternative, popularized by software developers, are so-called exploration days. The idea here is to allow your staff to come together and experiment with any crazy notion they dreamt about. Although the practical outcomes might not always be useful, these days provide a great opportunity to engage and motivate team members; allowing them to develop, self-educate and find their purpose within the organization.

The third building block for team competence is the *team's internal communication*. This is probably the most important factor when it comes to having competent teams, but also the one teams struggle with the most. When it comes to communicating effectively, we should focus on talking more and talking better through face-to-face communication as well as the power of establishing rituals.

The final piece of the building block puzzle is *creative tension*. This is the idea that individual team members look at the same thing from different perspectives and so come up with more innovative ideas. For this to work effectively, teams would need to be as diverse as possible. We are talking much more here than just gender balance. For a team to experience (positive) creative tension its members should come from different social/cultural backgrounds, have different levels of experience/education and so on. Anything goes really, although it would probably a good idea to not stress religious or political diversity as this rarely leads to positive creative tension.

Besides team diversity, roles in a team can also be used to encourage creative tension. Assigning roles such as *coordinator*, *challenger* or *thinker* to team members will help them challenge each other which in turn will heighten the creative tension. Crucial here is that the roles assigned are clearly outlined and that everyone understands the function of the different roles. If this is not the case roleplay might lead to negative creative tension.

There you are, four building blocks to help the novice, skilled and expert members you'll find in any team develop themselves and their teams to the best of their abilities. The question now remaining is how to identify which skills the team should develop. A popular Management 3.0 tool named the *competence matrix* can assist with this.

The Team Competence Matrix

The team competence matrix is a visualization of a team's strengths and weaknesses. This first column lists the competences the team needs to cover. The second 'RCL' column lists how many experienced (proficient) and expert (crackerjack) team members are minimally required to make the team function effectively. Subsequent columns show the names of the individual team members.

Let's riffle through at an example from Naked Espresso's Back of House team to see what this might look like (figure 12).

Team Competence Matrix

	RCL	Pierre	Cedric	Carmen	Evelyn	Zhifeng
Culinary Expertise	● 1 / 2	●				○
Inventory Mgmt	● 1 / 2	●	●	○		○
Health & Safety	● 1 / 4	●			●	○
Cooking Tech.	● 2 / 3	●	●			○
First Aid	● 1 / 2		○	○	○	

● = Crackerjack   = Proficient   ○ = Greenhorn

Figure 12: Back of House Team Competence Matrix

Once the team's required competence levels have been decided upon, every team member marks the skill level they think they are at for each of the competences. Now, with one glance, we can see which skills are lacking and what the appropriate measure for improvement might be.

In the example above, you can see that rows one and two are looking good, but in rows three and four Zhifeng needs to be brought up to speed for the team to meet their RCLs. Fortunately, both of the rows have crackerjack team members and so Zhifeng's training can be handled in-house, on the job. Row number five, on the other hand, is more worrisome and will need the assistance of an external expert to have the team trained up and meet the required competence level.

Improving Individual Competence

Besides leading by example, as mentioned previously, managers should also encourage their staff to study by themselves. This does not mean, however, that you should expect them to sacrifice their precious free time to become better employees for you, though. Instead, it means that you give them *time*, *resources* and *space* for study during their worktime.

Time here means that part of your staff's working hours should be allocated to self-study. As a general rule of thumb, most progressive organizations adhere to the 80-20 principle which means that 20% of an employee's working hours are allocated to training purposes.

Giving resources means that you should have materials available or at least have a budget for staff to buy the materials they need for their self-study. You can't reasonably expect people to pay for their own learning if it directly benefits your business.

Finally, giving space. This is not so much about creating physical spaces for learning (although you should do that as well), but about trusting people to study unsupervised. Experience shows that if you trust people to do something or behave in a certain manner, they tend to do it.

An Obligated Annual Learning Goal

Being a service provider and operating on a shift roster, the management at Naked Espresso had to juggle a bit with the ideas behind enabling self-study to make it work. Naturally, they can't afford a member of the team on shift to hide away in a corner with a book while customers are waiting. So, instead of allowing staff to use 20% of their individual work hours for self-study, the café has allocated 20% of total work hours for workshops that everyone can volunteer (but is not obligated) to join. With a bit of flexibility in scheduling and time swapping, they can make it work most of the time.

One interesting practice they have implemented at the café to create a culture of continuous learning is that of the *'Obligated Annual Learning Goal'*. When new members of staff are hired, they are asked to decide on a specific skill they intend to learn over the coming year. This skill doesn't have to relate to their work, it can be anything they are interested in: learning Spanish, salsa dancing, *Tai*

Chi, Japanese cooking, anything goes. Then, after a year, on the anniversary of their employment, they are to reflect on how things went and set a new goal. There are no repercussions if they don't meet their goals. The whole purpose of this practice is to foster the culture of continuous learning and keep employees interested in other things than work and thus effectively alleviate stress.

In addition to the annual personal review, the café also organizes a themed team-building day once a year during which everybody, from CEO to the freshest greenhorn, shares and celebrates their learning journey.

Learning from failure and experiments

Besides creating and fostering a culture of continuous learning through self-study, in-house training and external certification programmes, you also want to create a culture of experimentation.

In today's creative economy,* organizations and their employees need to be learning continuously to keep up with the pace and the best way to do this is through experimentation. But to be successful these experiments need to be run in a safe-to-fail environment. Also, what does success mean when running an experiment?

---

* The precise definition of the *creative economy* continues to evolve, but here it refers to work environments in which employees need to continuously adapt to new technologies, ways of thinking, social norms etc.

Well, success means failing at least 50% of the time. If most of your experiments succeed, you're not trying new ideas, you're just proving existing ones. As Thomas Edison once audaciously remarked, when reflecting on his many 'failed' inventions, "I haven't failed; I just found 10,000 ways that don't work."[57] In other words, you should expect the experiments to fail and make sure they are survivable. There's no point in running experiments that might bankrupt you. More importantly, you should make sure you (and your staff) know when an experiment has failed. The temptation to give something one more try, because too much money and time have been invested in it already, is often irresistible. Don't do it. Know when to stop.

The After-Action Review

An effective way to learn from experiments is to apply the so-called After-Action Review, a debriefing technique originally developed by the US Army.[58]

The way it works, very simplified, is that after running an experiment, the team members come together and answer the following four questions:

What did we set out to do?

What actually happened?

Why did it happen?

What did we learn from it?

You always need a plan of action and so you should always know what it was you set out to do. Even though things rarely go according to plan, the reason for having a plan in the first place is that you need a starting point to deviate from.

When things didn't go according to plan *(remember to expect 50% failure)*, work out why. But stay with the facts, no finger-pointing, no explaining away what happened because of unforeseen circumstances.

Next, evaluate your actions and work out why things happened the way they did. Again factual, no finger-pointing.

Finally, what did we learn from it? A concise but clear lessons learnt statement. Mistakes happen and as long as we learn from them that's okay. As the saying goes, "Only a fool steps into the same hole twice."

The WYSIWYG Kudos Wall

"If you water flowers they flourish, if you praise people they flourish," is a piece of advice business magnate Sir Richard Branson gives to aspiring entrepreneurs.[59] And it's true, everybody loves to hear they are doing a great job, but what if they don't? This was the premise of Maria's experiment I mentioned in the previous chapter.

What she was aiming for was a feedback system in which the customers would be able to not only express their contentment by, for example, leaving a small tip on top of the service charge but also any discontent they might feel.

To achieve this, she first tried the Management 3.0 practice of *kudo cards* and a *kudo box*.

The idea here is that handwritten kudo cards, as physical tokens of appraisement, are deposited in a box. Then once a week this box is emptied and the cards are given out to the appropriate recipients; time for a celebration.

But this first attempt didn't quite work out as she hoped. To be honest, I think this was to be expected as she had just copy-pasted the practice as described in the book *Managing for Happiness*.[60] The word kudo(s) comes from the ancient Greek κῦδος, meaning praise. For this reason, the kudo cards are all printed with phrases of praise, not criticism.

Figure 13: Kudo Cards © Management 3.0

Another setback she encountered was that, although the staff was quite enthusiastic about the idea, most customers just couldn't be bothered to write kudo cards and deposit them in the anonymous box near the door on their way out. But well, one learns through trial and error.

For her second try, Maria explored the Management 3.0 practice of the *happiness door*, a more out in the open evaluative tool. The happiness door (or wall, or board) combines the well-known practices of the *feedback wall* and the *happiness index*. On a feedback wall, people can pin notes with written feedback whereas a happiness index is a tool that measures the overall happiness of a group of people. This is normally expressed in either a percentage or a numerical scale (e.g. 1 to 5). A happiness door mixes the two by making room for feedback notes in a grid vertically divided into levels of happiness, often symbolized by smileys (figure 14).

Figure 14: Happiness Board

However, this didn't work either because, although now more customers were leaving feedback, the board distracted the staff too much. Whenever cards appeared in the bottom section of the board, it was all they would talk about and a game of defensive finger-pointing would commence. A balance between the first and second iteration had to be found.

For her final effort, Maria settled upon the emoji cards I described in the previous chapter. The main change she made was that there were no levels of happiness outlined on the wall anymore. Customers could just stick their cards wherever they pleased and this took away a lot of the distraction and anxiety among the staff. Moreover, with the previous happiness board, customers tended to copy each other. If, for example, early in the day a customer would put a note in the bottom part of the board, most of the feedback that day would be negative. If, however, the first note was positive, then so would be most of the other feedback that day. By eliminating the categories, Maria had also taken care of the customers' copycat behaviour.

Helping Each Other

Besides developing their individual competence, it's also essential for team members to help each other if they wish to improve the competence of the team as a whole.

At Naked Espresso they have put in place a number of routines to make this work. First and foremost, all new staff, no matter how experienced they may be, is buddied up with a *proficient* or *well-versed* team member to learn the ins and outs of how things are done at this particular café. Besides this, *crackerjacks* run regular mini workshops to improve the basic skills of their teams. Finally, there's a policy of 'free exploration' which means that staff members are encouraged to bring in and try out new food or drink recipes.

Team Communications

As I said earlier, a team's internal communication is probably the most important factor when it comes to their overall competence, but also the one teams struggle with the most. As we've been given more and more tools to encourage communication, our actual ability to effectively communicate with each other seems to have deteriorated. From typing short messages using made-up and confusing abbreviations to sending those messages to someone sitting right next to us, the art of casual conversation isn't quite what it used to be. Both in our personal and professional environments.

I would argue that, when it comes to communicating effectively, we should focus on talking more and talking better through face-to-face communication as well as using the power of establishing rituals.

To be honest, at a relatively small coffeehouse like Naked Espresso face-to-face communication isn't really an issue. Even though the staff work in shifts, these shifts overlap and rotate so everybody gets to see each other all the time. We did make some effort to create a ritual, though.

Rituals like a pilot's pre-flight checklists, daily Scrum stand-up meetings or Friday after-work drinks are habit forming and thus play an important role in creating an organizational culture.

The Niko-Niko Calendar

The ritual I had in mind for the Naked Espresso Café was the Japanese *Niko-Niko Calendar*. This *'with a smile'* calendar is a beautifully simple visualization of a team's overall mood.

Basically, it is just a grid with the columns representing days/dates and the rows listing the members of the team (figure 15).

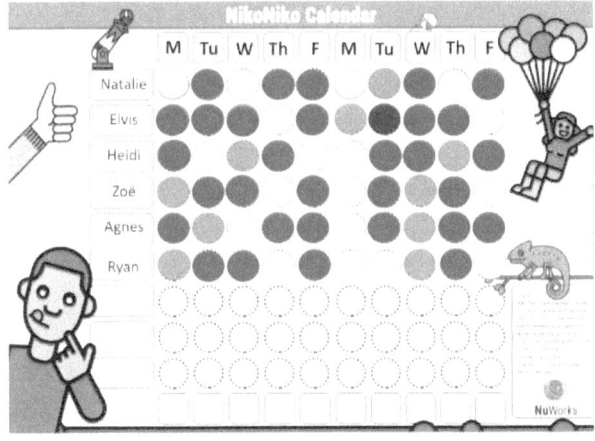

Figure 15: Niko-Niko Calendar © NüWorks

At the end of each workday, the team gathers around the calendar and scores their day by choosing a coloured sticker representing their mood. A green sticker indicates it was a good day, a yellow one *meh* nothing to write home about and a red one indicates one of those days you know you should've stayed in bed!

A communicative strong point of this practice is that as the team members put their stickers on the calendar at the end of the day, they explain to each other why they chose a specific colour. However, as the staff at Naked Espresso work in shifts, this wasn't really possible.

Instead, we decided to hang the calendar on the staff toilet together with a notebook. Now, while reflecting on their day during a toilet break near the end of their shift (it's a great place to think), staff members will put a sticker on the calendar and write a journal entry in the notebook to explain their choice of colour. Their reasoning can be either work-related or of a more personal nature, it doesn't matter as long as they explain why they feel how they feel. Whether they had a good or bad day, they use the power of the written word to close it off, go home and start afresh the next day and let it go.

The real strength lies in the visual part of the calendar. With one glance, a manager (or anyone else) can gauge the mood of a team. This visual power, combined with the insights provided by the moving motivators tool discussed earlier, can help managers create the best possible work environment for their teams. It's no wonder that some Japanese corporations have walls with months, if not years, of Niko-Niko Calendars to visualize how their workers' happiness evolved over time.

Creative Tension

Although effective communication might be the most important factor for team competence, making sure there's some creative tension in the team is essential as well. This is the idea that a team looks at the same thing from multiple different perspectives and so comes up with more innovative ideas.

For this to work effectively, teams need to be as diverse as possible. Again, this is much more than just gender balance. This diversity should be kept in mind when hiring new staff but with existing teams it can be created by making teams semi-stable (see chapter three).

Besides team diversity, roles in a team can also be used to encourage creative tension. Assigning roles to team members, will help them challenge each other which in turn will heighten the creative tension. Crucial here is that the roles assigned should be clearly outlined so that everyone understands the function of the different roles and negative creative tension is avoided.

In my opinion, there are five roles that should exist in any team to maximize creative tension.

They are: the *Coordinator*, the *Challenger*, the *Executor*, the *Thinker* and the *Liaison* (figure 16).

Let's explore how these different roles might positively affect creative tension and thus improve the team's overall competence.

Roles in a Creative Team

Figure 16: Team Roles © Management 3.0

The coordinator is the role assigned to a team member who will ensure the team has clear objectives and makes sure everyone is involved and committed. It is not a synonym for a team leader (if so he/she would just be bossy). Instead, the coordinator is an equal team member who outlines and prioritizes the tasks and keeps an eye on the bigger picture.

The challenger is one of the more interesting (and annoying) roles a team member can play and is the one who queries effectiveness and presses for improvement and results. He/she is the critical thinker who always questions why something is done a certain way or why it is done at all. If this doesn't happen, there's a great risk of getting stuck in bad routines just because, "that's the way we've always done it." If a team lacks someone who does this naturally, it's a role that should be assigned.

The executor is effectively the eyes on the ground for the coordinator. He/she is the timekeeper who urges the team to get on with the job in hand and does practical tasks. Especially when a team has an effective challenger, the executor is indispensable to make sure things get done. In a small team, the coordinator and executer roles could be assigned to the same person.

The thinker observes the team, weighs up the teamwork and suggests improvements. He/she is the creative thinker who not necessarily challenges the way things are done but tries to see if there's a better way of doing it. Ideally, the thinker observes the team (but also is an active team member) as they work and leads an evaluation afterwards.

The liaison is more or less a social coordinator who eases tensions and upholds communication within the team. With an effective challenger on the team, who stirs things up, a neutral mediator is always useful. The liaison is also the point of contact between teams to assure transparency of communication.

The Gadfly

When I introduced the concept of team diversity and roles to the Mezzanine, it caused quite a stir. This was not something they had ever even thought of. Weren't they just running a coffeehouse? But after some discussion they were willing to experiment with the idea.

There are two teams at Naked Espresso (if we exclude the owner-managers in the mezzanine). The Front of House consisting of Natalie, Elvis, Heidi, Zoë, Agnes and Ryan, somewhat micromanaged by Maria and then Cedric, Carmen, Evelyn and Zhifeng in the Back of House overseen by *Chef de Cuisine* Pierre.

When we began our experiment, the Front of House operated in three eight-hour (overlapping) shifts of two staff members. From 09:00 to 11:00 and from 19:00 to 20:00 there would be two people in the house to open and close the place whereas between 11:00 and 12:00 and from 17:00 to 19:00 there would be four people on staff. During the café's busiest time, from 12:00 to 17:00, a total of six staff would roam the floor.

Position wise, the Front of House was quite rigorously organized. Natalie, Elvis and Zoë were the baristas whereas Heidi, Agnes and Ryan were cashiers/waiters.

Compared to the Front of House, the Back of House had a slightly more easy-going schedule of two eight-hour shifts, overlapping during the 12:00 to 17:00 busy time, with no specific positions. This aside though, kitchen staff Cedric, Carmen, Evelyn and Zhifeng were kept on a tight leash by iron-fisted Chef Pierre Tang Yeu-weng.

To successfully move the café into a Management 3.0 environment, the Front of House needed the most work. The first change we decided to make was to get rid of the fixed positions. Instead of being a barista, cashier or waiter, all Front of House staff would now be cross-trained to fulfil all positions. This would make the work more varied (and thus more interesting/motivating) and would make scheduling a whole lot easier.

Next, I asked Maria to take a step back and trust her team. How to build this trust and delegate your responsibilities efficaciously is something I'll discuss in chapter four. For here it suffices to say that Maria, albeit reluctantly, agreed.

Then the team roles. It didn't make much sense to assign team roles when only a couple of staff were on shift, but between 12:00 and 17:00 all three teams would be present. So, we decided to have the teams self-organize during that timeframe when it came to the roles of coordinator, challenger, executor and thinker with the prerequisite that the roles were to rotate throughout the week. For the role of thinker, we stipulated that it had to be someone from the late shift (coming on duty at noon). The reason for this was that I wanted the thinkers to file a report of their findings each day. The role of liaison I reserved for Maria to give her some stake in the team.

The situation was similar for the Back of House which operated in two eight-hour shifts with all staff present between 12:00 and 17:00. The difference with the Front of House team was that Chef Pierre would be both the coordinator and liaison for the team whereas the roles of challenger, executor and thinker would rotate among the staff. Here also the thinkers should come from the late shifts so that they could report on their findings.

After a couple of months, we evaluated the changes and the overall feedback was quite positive. The role of challenger had had a bit of a rough start as many of the employees were uncomfortable with questioning everything that was done the way they had always done it. But over time they got more comfortable with the concept and even started enjoying being 'the gadfly.' *

One change that had come out of this was that the café had always required one of the Front of House staff to be present on the first floor's coworking space. One day Heidi, as the challenger, wondered if there wasn't an alternative possible to relieve the mostly idle staff on the first floor and put them to better use. Sean, overhearing the conversation, then recalled reading something about a

---

* Philosophically speaking, a gadfly is someone who is an annoyance to others because they provoke them through constant criticism, forcing them to think in unconventional ways.

wireless restaurant paging system. To cut a long story short, today the café has a Wi-Fi button on every table/desk with which customers can call for service, thus eliminating the need to always have a staff member present on the first floor.

A lot less enthusiastic were the employees about my requirement for thinkers to report on their findings every day. As most of the work in both Front and Back of House is fairly standardized, they felt there wasn't enough to report on other than repeating the words of the challengers. To meet them halfway, it was decided that the thinkers of a particular week should meet up on Friday afternoon and together produce one report for the week as the main role for the thinkers was to create a habit of reflection rather than instigating change. To help them keep track of their observations, we also devised a kind of scorecard.

Sometime after our evaluation, with the hierarchy flattened and the teams more flexible and self-organized, I sat down with Maria and Pierre and asked them how they felt about the changes we had made.

[Maria Suen Ming-ngai]: "For me, there are plusses and minuses. I think the team roles are working quite well and, as we can see from Heidi's example, it sometimes really creates good benefits for the shop. I also like being the liaison for the team, compared to before, I feel the staff tell me more and are also more willing to listen to me.

"But I find it hard to keep my distance from the team and just having to trust them. Sometimes I can see a mistake Agnes or Ryan will make long before they've even started the work. And I'm supposed to just let it happen? That I find very difficult."

[Pierre Tang Yeu-weng]: "That's exactly why I insisted on being the Coordinator of my team. I mean, it's all good and well this trusting the team, but to be honest I don't trust them enough to coordinate my kitchen. We can't have customers complaining just because we want to make our staff happy, now can we? Maybe over time, but not right now."

[Maria]: "I think I agree with Pierre, I'm quite sure these changes will work, but it's too soon to tell."

[Pierre]: *"Zhèngquè!"* *

---

* 正確 – *Zhèngquè* means 'right' or 'correct.'

3

Grow structure

"The tension of our time is that we want our firms to be flexible and creative but we only know how to treat them as systems of boxes with a limited number of arrows between them."
~ Esko Kilpi

As mentioned before, Management 3.0 isn't a fixed framework like Scrum or Six Sigma. Likewise, even though the main goal is to make organizations more agile, you can't just copy-paste the principles of the *Agile Manifesto* and claim you've reached Management 3.0.[61] So what should you do then?

The answer lies in picturing your organization as a city in which some parts emerge bottom-up while others are designed top-down. Management 3.0 proposes an appropriate mix of traditional top-down and more modern bottom-up approaches to managing your organization. To use a cliché, you need to think outside of the box provided by a fixed framework.

I should probably warn you that this chapter is going to be rather theoretical and abstract as most of the content doesn't really apply to a small organization like a coffeehouse. But, as it is part of Management 3.0 thinking, I think it should be included in this case study anyway. How? Let's see.

The 20,000 Feet Perspective

I used to skydive and trust me, viewing the world from 20,000 feet, heading towards the surface at a dazzling speed, really puts things into perspective.

Before you can get down the nitty-gritty of team organization, you should have a look at the bigger picture of the organization as a whole.

First of all, you'll need to balance *hierarchies versus networks*. A hierarchy relies on rules and processes which in turn create predictability and allow the formation of best practices. Hierarchical structures are suitable for those parts of an organization which rely on highly specialized work. For example, a finance department.[62] Networks, on the other hand, rely on collective intelligence. The different ideas and perspectives of a group of subordinates often prove to be more innovative than those of a group of executives in a boardroom. Therefore, networks are more suitable for less specialized departments of an organization like, for instance, a factory floor.[63]

Another subject to take into consideration is the balance between *specialization and generalization.* Since the 1960s, most work has been knowledge-based, but with the emergence of the creative economy this has changed. Pure knowledge work like accounting still requires specialization, but most other work needs a more generalized approach.[64] As most organizations today function like complex adaptive systems, many of us find ourselves doing things we've never had to do before and, consequently, weren't trained for. We need to innovate constantly and innovation is incompatible with specialization.[65]

Next, you should focus on which parts of your organization rely on *efficiency* and which ones on *effectivity*. Efficiency is primarily about inputs, the use of resources and costs whereas effectivity puts the spotlight on outputs, products or services and revenues.[66] As an example, you would probably want a procurement department to be efficient and a sales department effective. Efficiency tends to thrive in predictable, stable hierarchies while effectivity will do better in networks.

Finally, you should compare *centralization and decentralization*. Organizations with centralized decision makers tend to be more coordinated, limit waste and have lower average costs.[67] Decentralized decisions, in contrast, are made much quicker and probably more suitable in the ambiguous and fast-changing contexts of the creative economy.[68]

Although it might sound counterintuitive, it is possible to be centralized and decentralized at the same time. For example, SAFe* makes use of decentralized Scrum teams with centralized support services.[69]

Once you've picked and chosen which elements are suitable for which parts of your organization, you should end up with an organizational structure which is neither purely hierarchical nor a flattened network. You should have an ambidextrous organization or what the emeritus professor of Leadership at the Harvard Business School, John Kotter, calls a "Dual Operating System."[70]

---

* SAFe, *the Scaled Agile Framework*, is a set of organization and workflow patterns intended to guide enterprises in scaling lean and agile practices.

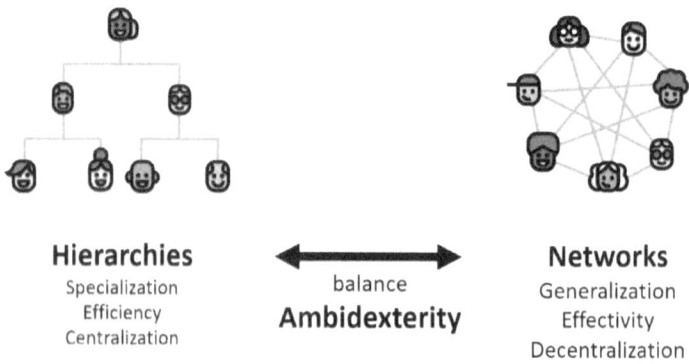

Figure 17: Organizational Ambidexterity © Management 3.0

The Close-Up View

With the organization as a whole balanced out (we'll look at how Naked Espresso did it in a bit), now let's have a look at team organization.

According to Professor Leigh Thompson of the Kellogg School of Management, a team is, "a group of people who are interdependent with respect to information, resources, knowledge and skills and who seek to combine their efforts to achieve a common goal."[71] It all begins with the team members.

To be able to work together effectively, the team members need to be skilled and have some expertise. Ideally, these skilled and expert individuals will be *T-shaped*, as mentioned in a previous chapter. A good example of this might be an army infantry group (10 soldiers) in which every group member has two specialized skills — for example, machine gun operator and first aid provider — but also has experience with all the other skills required to make the group function and so they can continue to function even if individual members are taken out. (A professional hazard I'm afraid.)

Traditionally, workplaces are organized vertically, i.e. each group is separated by speciality, safely tucked away in their own silos. The sales team in one silo, the marketing team in another. However, while the functions of each of these departments are inherently distinct, their goals should be consistent to avoid 'waste'. For this reason, an ambidextrous organization should organize its staff in *cross-functional teams around a value stream*, supported by shared specialist units.

Cross-functional here means that the team consists of members coming from different functional areas within the organization who work together to achieve a common goal. In other words, a semi-autonomous unit working on one value stream which in itself is just a series of activities creating a flow of value (i.e. a product or service).

To visualize this, you could compare it to Michael Porter's *Value Chain* concept in which an organization's activities are divided into primary and support activities.[72] The cross-functional teams focus on the primary activities (value stream) whereas the specialist units provide support (figure 18).

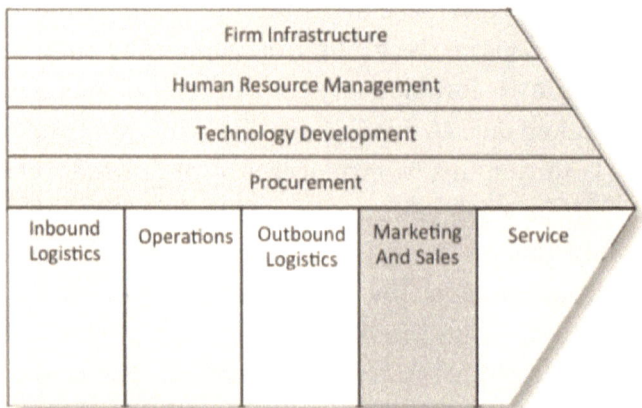

Figure 18: Michael Porter's Value Chain © Jinhyo Joseph Yun

Although you want to make sure a team has all the members required to be fully cross-functional, you should *keep it small* as a team becomes less productive as the size of the group increases (known as the Ringelmann Effect).[73] As to what the best group size is, well that depends. In Scrum a team is identified as 6 +/- 3, whereas an army fire-team consists of three soldiers in a functional group of ten.[74] The optimum size may vary, most important is that the team can do all the tasks they are required to do.

Besides being cross-functional, you also want your teams to *be semi-stable*. Some experts will argue that teams should be kept stable for better productivity but others claim that you should swap people around for more innovation.[75] Again, what you need is balance. Regularly swap team members around but keep the core stable. In science, this is referred to as a balance between cohesion or coherence *(staying together)* and permeable boundaries *(letting things through)*.[76]

A more controversial Management 3.0 idea is that of *rethinking job titles*. They used to have value because they describe an employee's position and responsibilities in an organization, but over the years most job titles have turned into nonsensical ego boosters. What does a Senior Deputy Vice-President of Strategic Procurement really do? Also, The concept of a fixed job is all but obsolete in an ambidextrous organization and thus so are the job titles attached to them. Instead of job titles, an organization should define the different roles the employees have within the organization. Does this mean people shouldn't have job titles anymore? Nope, but see the title as a conversation starter to explain a person's role within the organization. If a cleaning lady feels more valued by being called a Domestic Engineer, then why not?

Then *open allocation*, an alternative process of team self-organization polarized by Sociocracy.* This is all about letting people choose what they work on and with whom. The American videogame developer Valve Software (of *Counter-Strike* fame) allegedly put wheels under their employees' desks so that they could easily move around and join

---

* Sociocracy, *aka* Dynamic Governance, is a system of governance which seeks to achieve solutions that create harmonious social environments as well as productive businesses.

different teams. Anarchistic as it may sound, open allocation is not a free-for-all, though. In fact, it actually increases individual accountability because no one has the excuse of being put on a bad project under a shitty boss. If you fail to make an impact in an open-allocation environment, it's on you. You had the same opportunities to succeed as everyone else.[77]

Another aspect to consider is that of *double-linking*. One of the roles in a team, as outlined in the previous chapter, is that of liaison. Besides being the team's social coordinator, a liaison also serves as an ambassador to connect teams. The idea here is that members of interdependent teams nominate liaisons to represent their interests in the decisions another team makes. This double linking ensures the flow of transparent information and increases the value the of information because different people filter it according to their own perspectives.[78]

Finally, a typical insight from complex adaptive systems research (see complexity thinking), which is to *allow local rules*. What this means is simply that teams should be allowed to differentiate themselves and operate according to their own rules, as long as those rules are in harmony with their environment and corporate culture.

Let's now, after all this theory, have a look at how we grew Naked Espresso's structure.

The Mezzanine Perspective

The 20,000 feet perspective for Naked Espresso was rather simple. The owner-managers had in unison decided to transform their shop into a Management 3.0 ambidextrous organization and so were more than willing to experiment. To comply with the *Companies Ordinance* of Hong Kong, the senior management structure had to remain hierarchical, i.e. there has to be a CEO (Melvin) and a Company Secretary/CFO (Kim), but otherwise, we could flatten the organization.

The first decision we made was to take the hierarchy out of the Front and Back of House teams, some of the results of which have already been discussed in the previous chapter.

As for the Front of House, besides the staff now being cross-trained and cross-functional, Maria did live up to her promise to take a step back and trust her team. Now, rather than being a micromanager, she more functioned as a coach and confidant for the team. It was an improvement both she and her team highly appreciated.

The situation in the Back of House was slightly different. Ever since French Chef Georges-Auguste Escoffier launched the modern brigade system at London's Savoy Hotel in the late 19th century, the chef has been the undisputed leader of the kitchen.[79] His kitchen might be a small one but Pierre, being classically trained, is still its chef.

Like with the Front of House, Pierre would be the team's liaison but he would also be the coordinator (but keep in mind, a coordinator is not synonymous with team leader). Otherwise, there were not to be any traces of a traditional brigade, no *sous chefs,* no *chefs de partie* or even *demi-chefs*, just kitchen staff. And, as with the floor staff in the Front of House, all kitchen staff would be cross-trained and cross-functional.

When it came to the separation of specialized and generalized functions, things were quite simple. At the Mezzanine, only the Company Secretary/CFO (Kim) and IT manager (Sean) were considered specialists while the others, even the CEO (Melvin), would be generalists. At the Front and Back of House, everybody was to be a generalist, with the exception of Chef Pierre.

The other elements were even more straight forward. The Mezzanine and Back of House would be centralized and focus on efficiency while the Front of House would operate decentralized and was all about effectiveness.

A little segue to extrinsic motivation and merit money. With the Back of House focused on outputs, the Mezzanine decided to run another experiment. Using Raymond Aaron's MTO goal-setting system, they asked the Front of House team to set a *Minimum*, a *Target* and an *Outrageous* goal for the number of cups of coffee they hoped to sell each month.[80] If they reached the minimum number, every owner-manager would contribute five of their monthly kudos points to the department. Should the team reach their target number, the contribution would go up to ten kudos points and in the unlikely occasion they would hit their outrageous number, each and every owner-manager would bestow 25 kudos points on the team. Just a fun competitive way to increase motivation.

[Melvin Lo Man-shui]: "I think those MTO goals are the best thing we've come up with so far. Our Front of House staff are young and so this kind of gamification really works with them. It's like *sing ne,* they really try to get above the minimum goal and we've got to spend those kudos points anyway, it's a clear win-win situation."

The House View

With both Front and Back of House staff set to be cross-trained and cross-functional, they could be

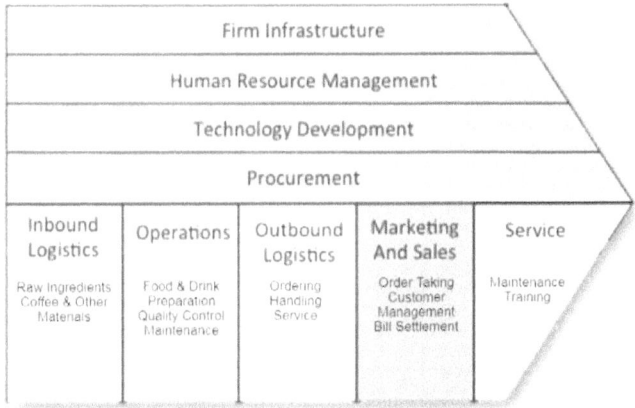

Figure 19: Naked Espresso's Value Chain/Stream

109

considered *T-shaped* employees. For the café's value stream, we created a basic value chain similar to both the Front and Back of House (figure19).

We didn't change anything regarding team size as the shift roster currently in place functioned fine, but we did make them semi-stable by suggesting (as an experiment) to once or twice a week swap some of the Front and Back of House staff members just so they could learn to appreciate each other's roles within the café.

We had already gotten rid of most job titles and created clearly defined cross-functional roles of both the Front and Back of House staff and the Mezzanine got started on working out their own role profiles within the organization.

The work at the coffeehouse doesn't allow any real open allocation as the teams were simply too small. But we did allow staff to decide who would have what role on their shifts (and if they couldn't work it out, there was always good old *Rock Paper Scissors*).

Finally, the double linking was covered by Maria and Pierre as team liaisons. And local rules, we decided this was also not that relevant but would be allowed if any came up.

4

Empower Teams

"Delegation is not a binary thing. There are more options than being a dictator or an anarchist. The art of management is in finding the right balance."
~ **Jurgen Appelo**

One of the great Catch-22s of business management is the issue of *What, How* and *When* to delegate. On the one hand, there are the managers who will often sigh they can't delegate a task because, "it's too essential that the objectives are met and things are done right and on time," and on the other are their staff who cry out they just can't get anything done because they are being micromanaged. So, who is right and what should you do?

Probably the biggest misconception about delegation, both from the managers and employees' perspectives, is that it is a binary option; either you delegate or you don't. This is not true but responsible delegation is difficult and managers often fear a loss of control when delegating tasks. Likewise, their staff sometimes have no idea how to deal with the responsibility for tasks delegated to them.

What's more, in their fear of losing control, those managers who do try to delegate tend to just hand over the reins and turn away, leaving their staff confused about what to do. The predictable result is that the team then won't live up to expectations and the manager loses trust in the idea of delegation altogether.

However, as they give the thumbs down to delegation, many managers will be predisposed to becoming micromanagers and micromanagement is what employees universally loath the most. Also, in complex adaptive systems (i.e. most organizations today) centralized control doesn't work because managers cannot possibly control everything required to have their staff successfully complete the tasks they set them.

A manager doesn't always know all the tedious details employees need to deal with to be able to get the job done and the employees often don't see the bigger picture of the tasks they are involved in. An employee has an incomplete mental model of the work and the same goes for the manager. But together they know everything, so if everyone just focuses on what they know and what they need to do, everything will run more smoothly and effectively. That is why it's best to distribute control throughout the organization and this unequivocally requires delegation, no matter how scary this idea might be.[81]

Distributed control, by management experts often referred to as empowerment, is an often misunderstood concept, though. As Professor Henry Mintzberg of the McGill University in Montreal puts it, "A good deal of what is today called 'empowerment' is really just getting rid of years of disempowerment."[82]

If we look at it from the binary perspective, it could be argued that on the far left side of the scale we find the authoritarian manager who says, "You are not allowed to do anything except what I tell you to do." They are the dictators (Management 1.0) who believe it's the managers who decide who's empowered and who's not. On the opposite side we find the precious snowflakes (Management 2.0) who say, "Go ahead, do whatever you want!" and believe everyone is empowered by default. The path to responsible delegation lies, of course, in the middle (Management 3.0) where a responsible manager would say, "You can do what you want except for the areas where I place some restrictions."[83]

The cause of the confusion about empowerment is that the word, like so many English words, has more than one meaning. Depending on the context, empowerment can either mean *to invest with power* or *to supply with an ability*. The 1.0 managers know and understand only the first meaning of the word empowerment (authority), while the 2.0 worldview favours the second meaning (ability). In most organizations, however, we need both which is why Management 3.0 aims for a more powerful work system, not better-controlled people.[84]

Moreover, authoritarian 1.0 management styles are counterproductive as most people entering the workforce today are better educated than their senior managers. And even if they aren't, knowledge about anything is only a few tabs on your phone away. It has become almost impossible to claim any authoritarian form of management control. Things change so fast these days that a superior's vast experience, once invaluable, also doesn't necessarily grant authority anymore.[85]

Effective empowerment is a reflexive relationship between equal partners and so, if we want staff to focus only on what they know and what they need to do, we need to replace the traditional corporate hierarchy. Instead of thinking of them as superiors and subordinates, we should see managers and their teams as control-givers and control-takers.[86] It might just be a matter of semantics but changing the tone from superiors and subordinates to givers and takers, sets the scene for mutual cooperation, respect and trust.

The 7 Levels of Delegation

Trust is what delegation is all about and so only by building trust can managers give away control and will their employees be able to take control. Successfully shifting from micromanagement control to fully delegated self-organized teams can be done in seven steps or seven levels of delegation: Tell, Sell, Consult, Agree, Advise, Inquire and Delegate.[87]

1. **Tell** means that the manager is the sole decision maker. It is the authoritarian 1.0 option where there's no room for discussion and no need for explanations. This level isn't appropriate for the modern workplace other than in situations of chaos where there's simply no time for discussion.

2. **Sell** is just a nicer version of 'tell'. At this level, managers still boss their employees around but at least they are trying to convince their teams that their decision is the best choice and help them feel more involved.

3. **Ask** is the level where actual delegation is starting to emerge. The manager still makes the decisions but will ask the team members about their opinions. However, this will only work if the managers truly listen to the ideas of the team and are willing and able to justify their final decision to everyone involved.

4. **Agree** is the level where managers and employees become equals. The manager is just a member of the team and all team members have an equal vote. The majority decides. This is probably the most crucial step in the delegation process as it will be the first where the manager relinquishes full control and only has one vote equal to the others and so authority shifts from the manager to the team.

5. **Advise** is the first level of delegation where the manager effectively gives control to the team. This means that the team makes the decision. If it's the wrong decision, the only thing the manager can do is change the level of delegation the next time. You might also have noticed that this level is the opposite of level three 'consult'. At level three the manager asks the team for their input and then makes a considerate decision. With 'advise', the team asks the manager for input but, in the end, they make the decision.

6. **Inquire** is the opposite of level two, 'sell'. The team makes the decision and, once consensus has been reached, 'sells' it to the manager. Like with 'advise', if it's the wrong decision, the only thing the manager can do is change the level of delegation the next time round.

7. **Delegate** means the managers leave the entire decision-making process to their teams. They don't even want to be bothered with the details, just see the results. Once managers have absolute trust in their teams, they can fully delegate the work. It will be a long process to get here but it's most definitely possible, although some responsibilities might never be completely delegated.

These delegation levels are naturally context-dependent so the 'right' level of delegation is always a balancing act. It will depend on the maturity level of a team and the impact of their decisions.

It might not be easy, but responsible delegation increases status, power, and order (see CHAMP-FROGS). Therefore, a system with distributed control will have happier employees and a better chance of survival in today's creative economy than a system with mere centralized control.

You might feel a bit dizzy after reading all that delegation theory. In fact, our brains are hardwired for visual information, so wouldn't it be a good idea to visualize these levels of delegation? The Management 3.0 tool *delegation boards* does just that.

The Delegation Board

A delegation board, sometimes referred to as an empowerment board, is an easy to implement tool which creates openness and transparency of expectations between managers and their teams.[88]

TASK	1 TELL	2 SELL	3 CONSULT	4 AGREE	5 ADVISE	6 INQUIRE	7 DELEGATE	8 WILDCARD	CONDITIONS

Figure 20: Management 3.0 Delegation Board

Basically, it's either a physical board or just a spreadsheet that vertically lists the key responsibilities that a manager might (or might not) delegate to his or her team. Horizontally, the board is divided into a number of columns, each of which represents one of the seven levels of delegation plus a 'wildcard' option (figure 20).

Ideally, managers and their teams would come together to identify the manager's responsibilities related to the team's work. Once these have been identified, the next step is to decide the appropriate level of delegation for each of those responsibilities.

Although there are no right or wrong answers to this, the question is: How do you decide the appropriate level of delegation? This is where the 'game' of *delegation poker* comes into play.

Delegation Poker

With delegation poker, every player has a set of eight cards, each card representing a specific level of delegation, plus a wildcard.* At the start of a round, the players are presented with one of the decision responsibilities to discuss. For example, "Purchases worth more than HK$ 1,000."

Next, the players privately choose the card which they feel best reflects how far they would delegate the decision-making process if they were the manager. Then, on the count of three, all players

---

* The 'wildcard' option is for those situations where levels one to seven don't suffice; the exceptions to the rule.

simultaneously reveal their cards. The choices made will (and should) probably be different, so the next step is to have those with the highest and lowest levels of delegation motivate their choices. This will lead to a discussion after which the group should come to a consensus about the most appropriate level of delegation for the task.

Of course, the intention of this game is not to side-line the managers, they will still ultimately decide on the levels of delegation they deem appropriate. However, playing this game with the team might reveal misconceptions and hidden assumptions from both the perspectives of the manager and the team members. It will create transparency and, therefore, lead to better end results.

Once a level of delegation has been agreed upon, this is marked on the delegation board (figure 21). When the delegation board is completely filled out, it has become a crystal clear visual representation of who is allowed to make what decisions.

TASK	1 TELL	2 SELL	3 CONSULT	4 AGREE	5 ADVISE	6 INQUIRE	7 DELEGATE	8 BOLDEBEO	CONDITIONS
Office hours						✓			
Vacation days			✓						
Project selection							✓		
Team membership					✓				
Salaries	✓								
Bonuses		✓							
Staff training				✓					
Equipment purchases						✓			

Figure 21: Management 3.0 Delegation Board, filled out

A more reflective and less gamified way to use the delegation board is to first have a manager ask the team members to mark the level of delegation they think a certain decision point is currently at. Next, they should mark the level of delegation they would like to see it at and connect the dots with an arrow showing the direction. Then the manager will do the same thing.

Probably their views will differ and so it will be time for some serious discussion. Once the smoke has cleared and consensus has been reached, both parties can agree on the level of delegation that will be set and fill out a board (figure 22).

TASK	1 TELL	2 SELL	3 CONSULT	4 AGREE	5 ADVISE	6 INQUIRE	7 DELEGATE	8 WILDCARD	CONDITIONS
Days off			●		✓	●			
Timetables					●	✓	●		

Figure 22: Example of an alternative Delegation Board technique.

Laying Down a Straight Flush

With the teams at Naked Espresso now flattened, self-organized and cross-trained, the time had come to set the appropriate levels of delegation. Let's see what the delegation poker game played by the Back of House team resulted in.

On a quiet afternoon, Chef Pierre and his team gathered around the kitchen table and discussed which responsibilities they figured should be listed on the delegation board. Then they played the delegation poker game and marked the outcomes of the discussions that ensued on a board (figure 23)

TASK	1 TELL	2 SELL	3 CONSULT	4 AGREE	5 ADVISE	6 INQUIRE	7 DELEGATE	8 BILDCRRD	CONDITIONS
Purchases < HK$1,000						✓			
Purchases > HK$1,000			✓						
Scheduling					✓				
Days off						✓			
Menu changes				✓					
Assigning team roles							✓		
Developing new team roles			✓						
Hiring/firing team members		✓							

Figure 23: Naked Espresso's BoH Delegation Board.

As you can see the first item on the board is purchases of less than HK$ 1,000. The team felt that this could easily be fully delegated, but Chef Pierre objected. His argument was that, although the amount might not be that significant, as the chef he should always know what was stowed away in *his* kitchen and not just find out about it from monthly cost reports. He didn't object against the delegation of the purchases themselves, and so it was decided to put the mark at level six, 'Inquire'.

Next, purchases above HK$ 1,000. Basically, with the same argumentation as the previous item, the team decided to take the opposite approach and opt for level three, 'Consult'. Chef Pierre assured the team that if he were to stock up on produce or equipment, he would first ask them if they needed anything or they could just come and tell him.

Then scheduling. Deep down, Chef Pierre agreed with the majority of the team who had played the number seven 'Delegate' card. His only concern was that, because of the still high staff turnover, more seasoned staff might bully new employees into accepting less popular shifts if the scheduling was fully delegated. For this reason, he pushed for level five, 'Advise'. The team would now have to ask for his input before going ahead which he felt would stop any wrongdoing. Somewhat reluctantly the team agreed.

Days off, the next item on the list was quite straightforward. Chef Pierre couldn't care less who took off when, as long as there would be enough staff in the kitchen. They should be adult enough to work that out among themselves he figured. But he did want to know who he could expect to find on shift, so level six, 'Inquire' was chosen.

Menu changes was an opportunity for some intrinsic motivation and so whereas most of the team suggested level five or six, Chef Pierre thought that they should work this out together with him as an equal team member, putting it a level four, 'Agree'. After some discussion, they decided to gather once a month to review the menu.

Assigning team roles was the first task everybody agreed should be fully delegated. At the start of a shift, the team would decide who did what without the chef's interference (or play *Rock Paper Scissors* if they couldn't work it out).

For the penultimate item on the board, developing new team roles, Chef Pierre was adamant that this was a task for management but that team input was welcome, so level three, 'Consult' was chosen.

Finally, hiring and firing staff. To everybody's surprise, here Chef Pierre audaciously threw down the 'Delegate' card. However, none of the other team members dared to burn their fingers on this responsibility. In the end, despite some witty arguments from the chef, it was decided to put the hiring and firing at level two, 'Sell'.

With the delegation levels now ranging from two to seven, it looked like the team had played a straight flush!

As demonstrated, with a completed delegation board everybody can easily see where they stand and what level of control they have for different responsibilities. As a result, everyone can now also be appropriately held accountable and so by distributing control not only employees will be empowered, but the managers as well.[89]

Ideally, as a manager, you'd want to delegate most team tasks beyond level four, 'Agree'. But this requires the right level of trust in the team.

There's one caveat I'd like to make about the 'Agree' level. Although it might seem the fairest and most democratic, it often isn't a particularly effective level. This is because with every team member having an equal vote, there's no arbiter and so discussions might go on forever and ever. Of course, there are some tasks which are appropriate for this level. For example, the menu discussion suggested by Chef Pierre can be set at level four because, although everybody might have their own ideas, they probably won't be so passionate about them that it would lead to endless hotblooded debates with knives drawn.

In short, when considering putting a task at level four, I'd first carefully look if it wouldn't fit better at levels three or five instead.

Training for Trust

To be able to trust a team enough to delegate responsibility, you need to be sure they will do the work assigned to them the way you expect them to do it and that the result will be what you were aiming for. To achieve this, you need to train for trust and there are essentially five steps to do this:[90]

> You do the work;
>
> You work with the trainee;
>
> The trainee works with you;
>
> The trainee works alone;
>
> The trainee trains someone else.

The first step (corresponding with delegation level one or two) is that you yourself, or an experienced member of staff you already trust, do the work and are observed by the trainee. This is to set the ground rules and have the trainee understand what will be expected of him or her.

Then in step two, you work with the trainee (delegation levels three and four). You still do the work, but now also ask the trainee questions to check understanding and, step-by-step, involve him or her more and more in the work.

When ready for it, you move to step three in which the trainee works with you (delegation levels five and six). At this level, the trainee will do the work but is observed by you (or an experienced team member). Every now and then, the trainees at this step should be spot-checked to see if they can explain what they are doing, why they are doing it and if they are able to justify any choices they made that differ from what they were trained to do.

When a trainee seems confident enough and has passed most of the spot tests, you can move to step four and let them work mostly unsupervised (delegation level seven).

Finally, when trainees have built up some experience, they should be allowed to train someone else to prove they have mastered their work and are worthy of your trust. This is a crucial step because, once they've earned your trust, they will do anything to not disappoint you.

Let's look at an example of Naked Espresso's Back of House to see how this might work out in practice.

The Path from Greenhorn to Proficient

When new greenhorns join his team, Chef Pierre will give them a quick tour of the kitchen and assign them their own workspace. As all staff are cross-functional, they won't be getting a specific station, just a place to put down their knives.

Once settled in, their in-house training begins in all earnest with the 'philosophy and system' of the *mise en place*, the workplace setup required before cooking.[91] Chef Pierre himself will show the new staff where to find all the tools and ingredients and then set up his own area for service, explaining the reasoning behind his particular *mise* choices as he goes along (step one).

Next, the greenhorns will be buddied up with a proficient or well-versed member of staff and for the next couple of weeks they will religiously set up their own workspaces exactly like Chef Pierre's, supervised by their buddy. Every now and then, Chef Pierre or one of the crackerjack staff might help them expand their *mise* setup depending on what they are required to work on (step two).

Once they're able to set up the *mise en place* figuratively blindfolded, they will be assigned work requiring extra tools or ingredients. As they add these to their workplace, Chef Pierre will ask them to talk him through their choices (step three).

Should they manage to pass the chef's prying cross-examinations, they will be given more freedom in the kitchen and more challenging recipes to cook (step four).

After an appropriate time, as they would have built up some relevant experience, they will be promoted to *proficient* and become the buddy of a new greenhorn (step five) and the circle reinstitutes.

To me, this internal training for trust procedure sounded good, but I was curious about what the staff thought about this. When I had a chance, I took Evelyn, who had only recently been promoted to Proficient, aside to find out.

[Evelyn Ng Ngaa-kei]: "To be honest, in the beginning it was extremely stressful. Everything I did was just wrong and Chef Pierre isn't a very patient man. He shouts a lot, but I guess that's just kitchen life, right? After some time it gets easier, though because you do the same thing over and over again.

"Probably one of my proudest moments was when the chef finally let me prepare the *Wind Sand Chicken*[*] for lunch by myself, and everything went just fine. We even got a happy emoji card with a 95% happiness score from the customers who had ordered it.

"Also quite nice with this way of training is that you kind of can go at your own pace. The chef won't move to the next level until you're ready for it. And because we're always having to explain why we do what we do, I really feel

---

[*] A crispy yet tender roasted chicken with a 'wind sand' texture because of fried garlic sprinkled atop, originally form Guangdong in China and well-loved by Hong Kong people.

like I'm learning. You know, the kind of hands-on stuff they don't teach you at culinary school.

"Next week I'm supposed to take over from Carmen as Zhifeng's buddy. I'm quite nervous about that but I guess the chef has put me in this position because he thinks I'm ready. I'll try not to disappoint him."

With a bit of discipline, it isn't that hard to train for trust. Also, be aware that discipline = freedom and helps to avoid micromanagement because, "when individual members of the team are highly disciplined, they can be trusted, and therefore allowed to operate with very little oversight."[92]

However, no matter how well your staff is trained and how much they've earned your trust, you still need to create clear boundaries for them. Unfortunately, most managers with a 1.0 or 2.0 mindset tend to forgo creating appropriate boundaries of control when delegating work.

So, the question for the 3.0 manager is, "How do you create the right boundaries?" And we'll look at that in the next chapter, align constraints.

5

Align Constraints

*"Happy employees ensure happy customers.
And happy customers ensure happy
shareholders — in that order."*
– Simon Sinek

A key concept of Management 3.0 is that an organization should be managed partly from the bottom up by allowing workers to self-organize (as discussed in chapter three). However, self-organization without clear boundaries can lead to utter chaos. Let me explain this by means of a diagram outlining the differences between alignment and self-organization (figure 24).[93]

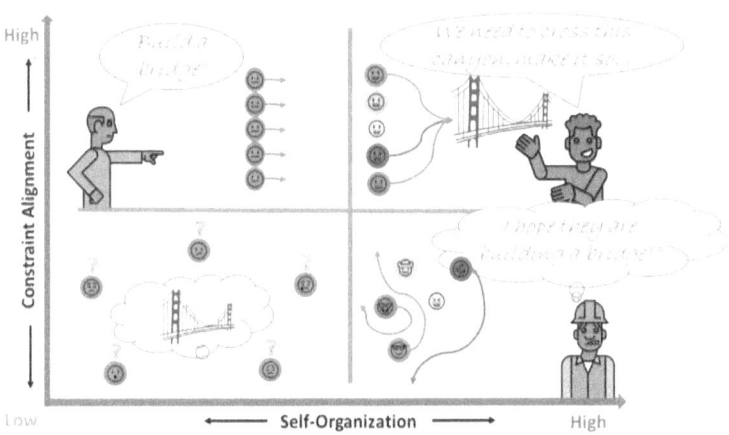

Figure 24: Alignment vs Self-organization.
Concept Hendrik Kniberg, illustration © Management 3.0

This diagram illustrates four different leadership styles based on team self-organization and the alignment of constraints. Constraint alignment here is mainly focused on the clarity of communication between a manager and the team as well as his or her ability to set clear-cut goals and objectives. The team's assignment in this diagram is that they need to somehow get across a canyon.

The bottom left quadrant symbolizes a team with low self-organization and low constraint alignment. Basically, this represents the micromanager who desperately wants to stay on top of everything and doesn't communicate well with the team. As a result, the team remains mostly in the dark about what is expected of them because the bigger picture (building a bridge) only exists in the mind of the manager.

The top left quadrant represents the management style most common today. The manager has a team of qualified and experienced team members and simply tells them what to do. The team will do the work and, when done, the manager will inspect the end result. This is Management 2.0

Then, the bottom right quadrant, which shows a self-organized team, but the kind we want to avoid. Each of the team members has their own specialization and experience and together, as a cross-functional team, they should be able to find a solution to cross the canyon. However, as communication is lacking and the manager hasn't set a clear goal, anything can happen. A self-organized team with low constraint alignment is really just a recipe for disaster.

Finally, the top right quadrant which represents the ideal Management 3.0 is aiming for, a self-organized cross-functional team with clear constraints. What makes this quadrant different from the top left one is that the manager doesn't tell the team what to do but instead introduces them to the task. Because of the diversity of the team's skills and experiences, they should then be able to come up with the best solution, even if this isn't a bridge. Whether the manager will accept their solution or send the team back to the drawing board will depend on the level of delegation that has been set for the task.

What this diagram makes specifically clear is that if teams are allowed to self-organize without clear boundaries, managing them becomes like riding a rodeo horse without any experience. It is therefore essential that a task (and an organization) has a clear purpose; a *reason d'être* that helps to point all the noses in the same direction.

We'll look at creating a clear purpose for tasks in a bit, but first I'd like to look at the why and how of organizational purpose.

At first glance, the benefits of organizational purpose are pretty straightforward. An organization with a clear purpose, will attract employees who believe in that same purpose and thus align themselves better with the organization. As a result, they will work harder and more effectively and because of that the business will make more money.[94] Simple right?

However, unless the organization's purpose has been carefully thought through, some issues might arise. For example, the people who identify with the organization's purpose, are also likely to agree on other matters and this could lead to a lack of diversity, causing people to think and feel the same about things. This, in turn, will stifle creativity. Another problem could be that managers might cop-out because, "everyone already knows what's expected of them." It's only natural to think that half the work is done once you've set an objective.

So, to reap the benefits of organizational purpose and avoid the pitfalls, your business should have a well thought through purpose, "which in some way contributes to a better world for some group of people, because if it doesn't, it will, and should, go out of business."[95] The question is how?

Having a 1,000 Songs in Your Pocket

For business owners, shareholders, board members and the stock exchange, the purpose of an organization is often just short-term growth and profitability. From a somewhat more philosophical perspective, however, it could be argued that the real purpose of any organization is the answer to the questions: "If my business didn't exist, what would the world be missing?" and "Why do we do what we do?" After all, if the sole purpose of an organization is growth then from a biological perspective it would just be called a tumour.[96]

An interesting point of view was put forth by British-American author Simon Sinek who, in September 2009, gave a now famous TEDx talk in which he argued that people are inspired by a sense of purpose (or 'Why'), and that this should always come first.[97] He based his search for purpose on a golden circle, a diagram of a bulls-eye with 'Why' in the innermost circle, representing people's motives or purposes, surrounded by a ring labelled 'How' which represents processes or methods. And all this enclosed by a ring labelled 'What' representing results or outcomes. Most businesses know what they do and how they do it, but not always why (other than the tumour of growth for profit).

A nice example of the 'Why' over the 'What/How' comes from Steve Jobs' introduction of the iPod in 2001. Although he did mention throughout his talk *what* it was (a portable music player) and *how* it worked (file types, memory, bit rates etc.), his main point was *why* they made it: because, "it's a thousand songs that fit right in your pocket."[98]

The *Ikigai* (生き甲斐) Venn Diagram

I figured that Naked Espresso, in their ongoing efforts to increase staff retention, should also work out their 'Why'. Finding or 'designing' the purpose of an organization is *the* job of management and the purpose they come up with should inspire and motivate all their employees. So I went up to the mezzanine asked the owner-managers what their reasons for running the coffeehouse were other than hard cash for themselves?

To find out, I opted for an alternative to Sinek's golden circle and introduced the Mezzanine to an approach inspired by the Japanese concept of *Ikigai* (生き甲斐), meaning "a reason for being."

To find your organization's *Ikigai,* you should envision a Venn diagram of four overlapping circles (figure 25).

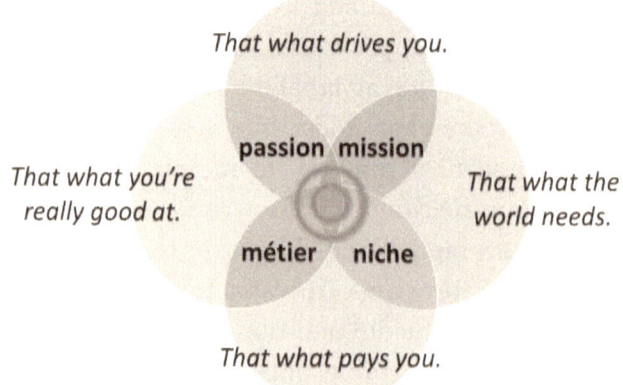

Figure 25: Ikigai (生き甲斐) Venn Diagram

In the left circle, you list all the things your organization is really good at and, in the top circle, you list all the factors that drive your organization. That's right, why you do what you do. Then, in the right circle, you list for which of the things you do there is a need in the market, that what the world needs. Finally, in the bottom circle, specify the things you do well, and for which there is a market, that what will make you money.

Once you've outlined the four circles, it's time to discover your passion, mission, niche and *métier*. The organization's true passion lies in the overlap of the things you're good at and that drive you. To find your mission, look at the overlapping topics in the circles of what drives you and what the world needs. Then, in the overlap of what the world needs and that what you get paid for, you'll find your niche in the marketplace. Finally, in the overlapping parts of the bottom and the left circles, you'll find your *métier,* your organization's most advantageous characteristic.

In the centre of the Venn diagram, where passion, mission, niche and *métier* all overlap, there you'll find the true purpose of your organization.[99]

Although it's not easy to create an *Ikigai* diagram for a business — after all, most businesses are just started to make money — it is an interesting thought experiment. I managed to convince the Mezzanine to give it a try and, after a long night, with many drinks other than coffee, they came up with the following purpose:

"To provide a comfy well-equipped workspace for digital nomads and start-up entrepreneurs and providing them with the essential caffeine, proteins and nutrients they need for their personal/professional growth."

Figure 26: Naked Espresso's Ikigai

135

Obviously, an *Ikigai* analysis basically results in a mission statement. All organizations today may have one, but the strength of *Ikigai* is that at least the mission statement has been thoroughly thought through by management rather than the marketing department.

Nurturing a Culture of Enacted Values

Now, with the 'Why' of Naked Espresso formulated, the next step was to cultivate an organizational culture in which the staff would thrive. This is not something that can be planned in a boardroom. You don't create a culture; it is the by-product of consistent exemplary behaviour.[100]

Inviting certain kinds of behaviour and discouraging others, is best done by defining clear organizational values that answer the questions: "Who do we want to be?" and "How do we want to act?" Another primary role of management is to instil these values in the teams and grow the culture.[101]

It is essential that the chosen values genuinely become part of the culture, otherwise your organization might end up like Enron* who famously had the values *integrity, communication, respect,* and *excellence* displayed in their corporate lobby.[102]

One way to espouse the values and envisioned culture throughout the organization is through a

---

* In case you don't remember, Enron was an energy-trading and utilities company based in Houston, Texas, that perpetrated one of the biggest accounting frauds in history.

culture book. Unlike a yawn-inspiring employees' handbook which is often top-down, bureaucratic and out of date, a culture book colourfully weaves together an organization's core values and explains the envisioned culture.[103]

At Naked Espresso, the Mezzanine is still working hard on a culture book. But they've already defined their core values, they are:

Treating all others the way we want to be treated ourselves;

Encouraging open and honest communication up and down the line;

Keeping things simple and real;

Delivering uncompromising quality and service with a smile;

Always staying relevant and at least one step ahead of our competitors;

Being the best version of ourselves we can possibly be.

Just writing down these values and hanging them on a wall in a nice frame isn't enough. As you will see in the next chapter, to ingrain these values into the culture they need to be continuously reinforced to stay top of mind. The best way to do this is through anecdotal stories which are often repeated to fortify the culture and should be made available to everyone.[104]

Besides the culture book in progress, the management at Naked Espresso created two other interesting approaches to boost their values. The first is that on the merit money app which staff use to reward each other (see chapter one), they need to tag one of the business' core values when they allocate points. In conjunction with this, the team is encouraged to share stories relating to the shop's purpose and values during the annual 'learning goals team-building day' (see chapter two).

Getting Things Done

Finding the real purpose and identifying the core values of your organization is one thing, giving a clear purpose to the work that needs to be done another altogether. One way is to set create clear goals, but how do you get the team to actually kick into gear and achieve those goals?

Setting S.M.A.R.T. Goals for the Team

Having been around since the 1980s, the concept of S.M.A.R.T. goals is probably quite familiar, but there's a reason it's been around for so long. Ideally speaking, goals throughout all parts of an organization should be:

Specific – they specify the who and what;

Measurable – they have clear indicators of progress;

Achievable – they can be done;

Relevant – they align with long-term plans;

Timeboxed – they have clear deadlines.

Specific here means that for any task it should be unambiguously clear who are involved, what you want them to achieve and, if necessary, what tools they have available to do it.

In addition to being specific, it's essential that the goal is *measurable*, i.e. the team should know exactly when the goal has been achieved. If a goal is more long-term, it will be useful to set milestones along the way to allow the team to re-evaluate and course-correct if needed.

As for *relevance*, this just means that the goal should be consistent with any other goals you've set for the team. If a goal doesn't contribute toward broader objectives, it should be reconsidered as it can easily become a distraction and break the flow of the team.

Finally, *timeboxed*. People (always!) procrastinate, so setting a clear deadline is crucial. Probably with some milestone deadlines along the way to keep the momentum going.

Let's have a look at an improved S.M.A.R.T. goal set for the Front of House at Naked Espresso. Originally one of the fuzzier goals set for the team was:

"To provide better customer service."

Reshaped as a S.M.A.R.T. goal this has become:

"To see the Front of House team increase their customer satisfaction score to at least 85% by the end of this year."

Unlike the ambiguous goal that went before it, this goal is S.M.A.R.T. because:

S: It is specific as it states that the Front of House team (who) should increase their customer satisfaction score (what).

M: It is measurable because it specifies an 85% score out of 100, a number which can be measured using the emoji cards.

A: This might not be easy, but it should definitely be possible to achieve the goal.

R: Customer satisfaction is 100% relevant to the success of a service-based business.

T: The goal is timeboxed, as long as someone keeps an eye on the calendar.

It is the combination of the objective and its action plan that is essential here. Therefore, serious management should focus on these twins and not just the objective.

Leading With Intent

Once a goal is clear, the next step is to get the team to act and achieve the goal. To do this, they must be set a task. And a well-defined task consists of four parts:

The task itself;

The purpose of the task;

The manager's intent;

The end state.

The task itself is the sum of the actions the team needs to take to achieve the goal. *The purpose* is an explanation of why the task is important and *the manager's intent* explains the manager's reasoning behind setting the task. The intent is essential because it will allow the team to pursue the goal in line with the manager's point of view even if things don't go as planned. *The end state*, finally, unambiguously articulates the desired end result.[105]

An example of a typical task at Naked Espresso's Back of House might look like this:

Task:
"For the morning shift to set up the *mise en place* for the lunch service…"

Purpose:
"… so that the kitchen staff on duty can transit into the busy lunch service without qualms."

Manager's Intent:
"I want my kitchen to be in tip-top condition at all times so that my staff can work in a natural flow. If the *mise* is set on time, everyone will be able to work without hiccups and thus provide the excellent service that is expected."

End State:
"I expect the *mise* for the lunch service to be fully *en place* by 11:30 sharp."

Note that this qualifies as a 3.0 task because it is left up to the morning shift to decide who will do what and how they will set up the *mise*. Also, timing is up to them as well, as long as they'll meet the 11:30 deadline as set in the task.

To get an idea about what the Back of House staff thought about the (hopefully) clearer goals and tasks, I took Cedric, one of the more experienced members of staff, and greenhorn Zhifeng aside and asked their opinions.

[Cedric Tsong Tou-yeu]: "Well, if I'm really honest, I don't see that much difference. I guess it's true that adding purpose and intend to the task makes things more clear. But most work in the kitchen is fairly standardized, it just needs to be done and we do it the way we've been trained. Having the chef add his intend really seems just symbolic to me."

[Zhifeng Wu Zeon-gwan]: "I disagree, I do think it makes a difference. Most of the time I don't really know what to do yet and so to know the chef's thinking is really useful. Also, before we were always told we should reduce food waste, but know we know that we should this by reducing our portion sizes by 10% for the next month. I find that really helpful."

6
Improve Everything

*"Because the people crazy enough
to think they can change the world,
are usually the ones who do."*
~ Steve Jobs

Now, with an ambidextrous organization and the teams energized, competent and empowered (with appropriate constraints), we should keep the momentum and make sure we keep improving everything.

To do so successfully, it is important to realize that creative workers are gradually replacing knowledge workers and so managers should nurture creativity rather than focus on hoarding knowledge.[106] The value of knowledge work is shrinking at an unprecedented speed as almost everything we need to know can easily be found somewhere in the 'cloud' through just a couple of tabs on a smartphone. With creative workers here I mean employees capable of adjusting to the ever-changing contexts at their workplaces without missing a beat. So how do you nurture creativity and manage your staff creatively? Let's find out.

Principles for Creative Management

The five principles listed here are simply 'stolen and tweaked' ideas taken from a great number of books on creativity and innovation.

> Nurture Diversity;
>
> Favour Coopetition;
>
> Rely on Merits;
>
> Optimize the Workplace;
>
> Optimize Constraints.

First *nurturing diversity*. As we discussed in chapter two, creative tension is essential to have teams work at the best of their abilities. Creativity managers dislike brains being the same as this will stifle creativity. They know that the most innovative products and services emerge when people connect ideas from entirely different contexts.[107]

Then *coopetition*, a portmanteau of cooperation and competition used to describe cooperative competition between individuals or functional units within the same organization.[108] To visualize this, you might think about professional cycling. In any given race, the frontman of a team will have a number of *domestiques** who will help him by riding in front of him, overtaking each other and thus creating a slipstream the frontman can benefit from. So, by competing for the front position, they cooperate

---

* *Domestique* are riders who work for the benefit of the team's frontman, rather than trying to win the race themselves.

to bring their frontman to an ideal position for the final sprint to victory. For Management 3.0 coopetition means that managers should replace hierarchical thinking with network thinking and rethink job titles by replacing positions with roles.[109]

As discussed in extrinsic motivation section of chapter one, *rely on merits* means that, managers should device their own creative merit money programmes to keep their staff motivated. But keep in mind, bonuses will only be effective if (and only if) the six rules of merit money are covered.

The physical environment has a huge impact on people's creativity and so *optimize the workplace* is all about creating surroundings that inspire creativity. You can do this by actively promoting a couple of things. First of all you should encourage 'play'. Unlike what most managers think, having staff wasting time in a fussball competition isn't a bad thing, it stimulates creative thinking. Other things to approve of are customization and adaptation the workplace. Don't be an office Nazi, if someone wants to move a desk, sit on a skippy ball or work standing up, why not? Finally, you should support 'escape', i.e. allowing staff to work away from the office. Don't think people won't work unless they are supervised. If they truly like their work, they'll work harder at home or a café than they would at the office.[110]

Lastly, *optimizing constraints*. This means that you should create an environment of continuous learning and exploration, not just focussing on results. When it comes to exploration, you might want to go as far as mandating experimentation, but keep in mind that any experiment should be survivable (see chapter two). In addition to this you should remove any *brules*. These are 'bullshit' rules that maybe once had a purpose but not anymore. Don't keep them just because, "that's how it's always been."[111]

There you are, five principles to manage any organization creatively. Let's now take a look at how this played out at the café.

Creative Management at Naked Espresso

As for nurturing diversity, this is a work in progress (see chapter two). One step that management has taken to forge more staff diversity is to introduce personal maps into the job interviews. As discussed in chapter one, personal maps are a magnificent tool to learn more about someone's personality. So now, before an interview, candidates are sent a description of the tool and asked to create their maps and bring them to the interview. Part of the interview is then conducted by going over the interviewee's map and the interviewer (Maria or Pierre) will pay specific attention to how he or she might diversify the team.

Coopetition at the café has been extensively covered in chapter three. Both the Front and Back of House teams are now self-organized and cross-functional and the teams regularly swap staff members to better appreciate each other's roles within the organization.

Naked Espresso's merit money scheme has been discussed in detail in chapter one. Suffices to say that it's a great fit for the café as it satisfies both extrinsic and intrinsic motivational factors. Besides this, the scheme has turned out to be a great monthly ritual, as well as an effective non-business ongoing teambuilding exercise.

More troublesome has it been to optimize the workplace. In the mezzanine, everybody has been able to optimize their desks to their hearts' desire, and at the first floor's coworking space monthly dedicated desk users are now allowed to customize and adapt their workspaces (within reason).

A café, however, is not an office and so doesn't really lend itself to personalization by individual staff members. In the Back of House there should have been more flexibility, but Chef Pierre is adamant that *his* kitchen is organized his way.

Finally, optimizing constraints. Through their 'Obligated Annual Learning Goal' and regular practical mini workshops the café has made a splendid effort towards creating an environment of continuous learning. Also, experimentation, although mostly work in progress, is encouraged in both the Front and Back of House and at least one *brule* (always having a staff member present on the first floor, (see chapter two) has successfully been removed.

Change Management

Trying to move an organization into the realm of Management 3.0 requires a lot of change and implementing any form of change is hard, very hard. In fact, according to a McKinsey study, nearly 70% of change management efforts fail.[112]

Change management is so difficult because one of the most persistent cognitive biases that plagues all of us is the 'status quo bias' aka the 'if it ain't broke, don't fix it' frame of mind. It's simply in our DNA to resist change and that's not so strange because, to be honest, far too often managers implement change and/or reinvent the wheel to fix things that 'ain't broke'.

Why Does Change Management Often Fail?

The main reason staff will prefer the status quo over change is that they often don't see the point; there's no sense of urgency. Unless there's an obvious need for change, why would they get onboard? Most of the time, the reason why they don't feel this sense of urgency is because nobody has pointed it out to them. This lack of communication often occurs because there's no dedicated team to lead the change in the organization.

Another reason why people don't see the point of change is because there's no clear vision. The path of change is dark and convoluted. Without a guiding light at the end of the tunnel, it's hard to take the first step and even harder to keep going. Unless a clear picture of the end goal can be painted in the minds of their staff, managers will have a hard time leading the change effort. Moreover, even if a vision has been formulated, oftentimes it will have ended up as a fluffy hollow phrase, hardly capable of inspiring even the most willing employee to act.

Speaking of which, for employees to take action and implement the required changes, they need to be actually able to do so. A factor often overlooked by change managers is that they need to empower their teams to act on the vision laid out before them. Also, properly empowered employees will need clear milestones or short-term wins to guide them through the darkness into the light.

Then even if, as a dedicated leader, you made your staff feel the urgency, painted a clear picture of the end goal, empowered your team and gave them measurable milestones, there is still another serious obstacle ahead. Even though it's almost two decades ago, I'm sure you can still recall the image of US President George W. Bush standing on the deck of an aircraft carrier back in May 2003 and declaring victory in Iraq... too soon. This tendency of declaring victory prematurely is one of the most perilous pitfalls for implementing change. Again, the path of change is long and uncompromising, there are no shortcuts.

A final mistake when it comes to implementing change in an organization is that the changes achieved aren't firmly anchored into the organization's culture; as a result they won't last. As the legendary management consultant Peter Drucker once put it, "Culture eats strategy for breakfast." [*]

"Just Do It!"

Although the reasons why change management efforts fail might be an interesting topic in and of itself, the real question that needs to be answered here is: How do you get change management to succeed?

Simply put, successfully implementing change and making those changes stick is an eight-step process which can be divided into three distinct phases. It all begins with creating a shared understanding of the difficulties lying ahead, followed by engaging and enabling the employees and finally implementing and sustaining the change achieved.

8 Steps for Successful Change Management

Establish a sense of urgency;

Form a dedicated change management team;

Formulate a clear relevant vision;

"Walk & Talk" the vision;

Empower teams to act on the vision;

Set clear milestones;

Consolidate improvements;

Institutionalize new approaches.

---

[*] The attribution of this quote to Drucker is actually contested, but that really doesn't change its value here.

Creating a Climate of Shared Understanding

As mentioned earlier, the main reason why the implementation of organizational change fails is resistance from employees who don't see the point. This is not always resistance on the work floor where any change is felt the most, but it could also be the intransigence of middle managers or even high-ranking C-suite executives. Most often this inflexibility is caused by a lacking sense of urgency combined with a lack of leadership and vision.

Therefore, the first step for successful change management is to *establish that sense of urgency*. It would probably be wise to point out here that a sense of urgency doesn't equate to a state of emergency. The latter is an after-the-fact response to an action or consequence, while urgency is a proactive state of performance created by management in which they alert the organization that change must occur.

To create a sense of urgency managers should clearly identify the affected stakeholders and 'sell' to them the dangers of the status quo. In effect, managers should create a compelling narrative that tells the stakeholders why it is not in their best interest for the business to stay in its current state. It is critical here that this narrative contains both a compelling picture of a desired future and the danger of accepting the status quo to avoid the creation of a sense of doom rather than a sense of urgency. This should be done through sharing relevant information with all stakeholders, and openly discussing the opportunities and threats they might face.

Clear communication in this phase is crucial and must be honest. An obviously manufactured sense of urgency will soon be seen for what it is and will lead to failure. To succeed here means that all stakeholders understand that change is, in fact, unavoidable.

The next step in this phase is to *form a dedicated creative change management team*. Successfully guiding an organization through a change process cannot be done as a side-hustle, it needs complete attention. For this reason, a team fully dedicated to the task is essential. Creative in this context means diverse. An effective change management team should not be only made up of senior managers but also stakeholders from every level of the organization. This diversity is necessary because all stakeholders will be affected differently, so only if all of them will have a voice in the team leading the change, the process can be completed successfully.

To paint a picture, racehorses wear blinders so that they stay focused and won't veer off course. However, change management isn't a race, it's a steady process. The required changes will only be accepted if all the different viewpoints are taken into consideration. This team diversity is even more important for the third step in phase one, formulating a clear and relevant vision.

Too often corporate vision statements end up as empty non-inspiring phrases, hidden away on a boardroom wall. The key to *a clear and relevant vision* is that it should contain a transformative story with a consistent 'what' and a 'why' resonating with the different stakeholders. The vision should be a descriptive tale outlining the journey of change the organization will embark on, justifying it with expected outcomes and relevant examples. An effective change vision expresses an understanding of the past, explains the present and shares the desirable future. Once a clear and relevant vision has been defined, the change management process can proceed to its second phase.

Engaging and Enabling the Employees.

Formulating a vision is one thing but avoiding it to go stale another altogether. The key here, once again, is communication. Printing out a long-winded fluffy vision statement and hanging it on a wall won't do. To begin, the vision needs to be boiled down to a simple catchy phrase for everyday use and should be free from any buzzwords and jargon. My personal favourite of all time, although not specifically related to change management, is Nike's iconic, "Just Do It."

This catchphrase should be everywhere, the consistent 'what' in stories, metaphors, analogies, and examples used to paint a compelling picture of the envisioned future for the employees and managers who need to be sold on the change. Another crucial step in communicating the vision is that the change management team needs to lead by example and *'walk the talk'.* In order to win the hearts and minds of all stakeholders, they need to continue the discussions opened up in phase one and address any issues that have come up to ensure the successful implementation of the change vision. If the change management team communicates the change vision with simplicity and repetition, engages all stakeholders in two-way communication and diligently addresses emerging issues, organizational change might still be difficult but not impossible.

The next step in phase two is to *empower teams to act on the vision*. Over time, organizational procedures, reward systems, performance measurements and so on, will have been formed to support the status quo. Given these dynamics, the change management team's communication efforts alone will be insufficient to make significant lasting change in the organization.

To make change happen, the change management team will have to evaluate existing systems and remove or adjust those hindering the change effort; there needs to be a breakdown before the breakthrough.

In addition to this, the organization needs to invest in training and development of employees at all levels. This is essential to enable the employees to embrace the change. Think of this step as going on a cross country road trip with an old car. The car might still be fine for short distances, but to take it on a long trip it needs to be checked out, minor repairs need to be made and certain parts might have to be replaced. Omit this and you'll likely find yourself stranded on a dark desert highway at some point, but with the right preparation it might just be the trip of a lifetime.

Phase two's final step is to *set clear milestones*. The road to successful change will be long and full of obstacles, it can be hard to keep the momentum going. Setting clear milestones will help with this. To continue the road trip analogy, milestones are like highway rest areas, they aren't your destination, but they are necessary if you plan to arrive at the destination in good shape. A clear milestone has to be unambiguously achievable, visible throughout the organization and directly related to the change effort.

Implementing and Sustaining Change.

To avoid losing momentum, the change management team must *consolidate the gains* from achieved milestones and implement more change. This should prevent the organization from reverting back to the old way of doing things and counter any continuing resistance to change. Change management fails when the process slows down before the change effort is completed. To avoid running out of steam, the change management team should maintain the sense of urgency throughout the process. They should not get too comfortable with early successes as people easily revert back to the old way of doing things.

The last, often overlooked, step for successful change management is to *institutionalize the change* into the organization. Few outcomes are worse than having devoted significant resources and time to an organizational change effort only to have the organization revert to its old way of doing things. This will seriously hurt employee morale and breed cynicism. Change won't last unless senior management aligns the organizational culture with the changes that have been implemented. It also requires everybody to stay engaged until the end. Senior management must anchor change into the organization if they want the change effort to become a lasting part of the organizational culture.

Leading change in an organization is not quick or easy, it requires preparation and perseverance. But with a systematic approach managed by a dedicated team it can most definitely be done.

Just in case you hadn't noticed yet, the process outlined here is my condensed interpretation of John Kotter's *Eight Steps Leading to Change* method.[113]

Change Management at Naked Espresso

Although this Improve Everything section is part of the final point of view of Management 3.0 change management, at Naked Espresso the eight steps previously outlined have been part of the process right from the start.

As the change process at the café was geared towards staff motivation and retention, both of which were suffering, a sense of urgency did not need to be created. The first step, therefore, was to create a dedicated creative change management team. In line with the recommendation to diversify as much as possible, it was decided that the team would consist of Melvin (CEO), Sean (IT), Natalie (FoH), Agnes (FoH) and Cedric (BoH).

Melvin was an obvious choice because, as CEO, he would have to sign off on any changes made. Sean, as IT-manager, was also obviously included because a properly functioning IT-environment is indispensable for the digital nomad part of the café and so they needed to make sure any changes proposed would not negatively affect the networks.

More interesting was the choice for the three staff members representing the Front and Back of House. Maria and Chef Pierre were side-lined because it was felt they would be too busy with their regular tasks to fully dedicate themselves to the change management team. Natalie and Cedric, both experienced long-term staff members, were the most logical choice to replace their managers.

Agnes was added to the team because, as a newly hired greenhorn, she would be the voice for the staff the proposed changes would be all about.

Then the vision. Like any business, the café has mission and vision statements for the outside world, but for the change management process they needed to create a clear and catchy vision for internal use. After a lot of discussion and fine-tuning, the team came up with:

> *"To help all our staff become the best they can be and motivate them to provide service with a genuine smile."*

Is it perfect? Nope, but at least it's focused on all the stakeholders and it has kind of a transformative story attached to it. A small tough I personally like is the use of the adjective 'genuine' before smile as genuine smiles are universally perceived as more sincere and honest.

As you have read in previous chapters, 'walking and talking' the vision has been extensively implemented in both the Front and Back of House through numerous experiments such as the kudos wall, MTO goal setting and delegation boards.

Together with making the teams more cross-functional and self-organizing, delegation boards have also been used to empower them to act on the vision. This, of course, is an ongoing process.

Setting clear milestones proved to be a more difficult task because the team didn't really know what to make of this. In the end, they settled on achieving the 85% customer satisfaction score, as mentioned in chapter five, as a milestone to indicate that service with a genuine smile has been achieved. Other milestones are still a work in progress.

When it comes to institutionalizing the changes into the organization, the team feels that this is being done by virtue of the continuous implementation of the Management 3.0 practices, as well as the story sharing element of the café's annual 'learning goal team-building day'.

In a nutshell, all three teams at Naked Espresso, the Mezzanine, Back of House and Front of House enthusiastically jumped into the deep end and allowed themselves to be surprised. The path may still be long and convoluted, but the light at the end of the tunnel is becoming brighter with each experiment the teams put through the test.

Since we started the Management 3.0 journey and created an environment of experimentation, no staff has resigned and the overall atmosphere at the café has improved significantly. Dare I say it… yes I do, "Mission accomplished."

Part III

Retrospective

After-Action Review

"There are no secrets to success. It is the result of hard work, learning from failure and persistence."
~ Colin Powell

As discussed in chapter two, the after-action review was originally developed by the US Army, but it has been a popular business tool ever since the Dutch-British oil and gas company Shell began experimenting with it in 1998. Nowadays, companies like Colgate-Palmolive and Harley-Davidson successfully use these reviews to identify both best practices and mistakes.[114]

Lessons Learnt

The implementation of Management 3.0 practices to help an organization become ambidextrous with energized staff who are competent and empowered is a steadfast process which needs constant reinforcement. The case of Naked Espresso is also ongoing, but after nine months of conducting various experiments, we decided to run an After-Action Review to gauge progress. Let me share the results of this review with you.

What Did We Set Out to Do?

The reason why the management at Naked Espresso wanted to try out Management 3.0 practices was quite straightforward. Inspired by the book *Managing for Happiness,* their aim was to:

> *"help all our staff become the best they can be and motivate them to provide service with a genuine smile."*

If we reverse-engineer the change process the café went through, we can see that they set out to:

1. Energize the staff by improving both factors of extrinsic and intrinsic motivation at the workplace by creating:

    1.1. A transparent four-tier salary formula;

    1.2. A *"Night at the Races"* monthly merit money scheme;

    1.3. Personal maps, to get to know and understand each other better;

    1.4. Moving motivator radar charts to better understand the teams' intrinsic motivators;

    1.5. Emoji cards with happiness scores for customer feedback (WYSIWYG Kudos Wall).

2. Improve the overall competence of the Front and Back of House teams, as well as that of individual members of staff by:

    2.1. Utilizing team competence matrices;

2.2. Introducing 'Obligated Annual Learning Goals' for all staff;

2.3. Encouraging experimentation;

2.4. Implementing a Niko-Niko Calendar;

2.5. Creating creative tension in the teams.

3. Make the organization ambidextrous and more self-organized and cross-functional by:

3.1. Flattening the hierarchy;

3.2. Specifying who should be specialized and who more generalized;

3.3. Specifying which departments should focus on efficiency and which on effectivity.

4. Empower the teams through responsible delegation and training for trust by:

4.1. Creating team Delegation Boards;

4.2. Defining clear career paths for the café.

5. Align constraints by:

5.1. Creating the café's *Ikigai* Venn Diagram;

5.2. Formulating the core values for the café;

5.3. Formulating S.M.A.R.T. goals for the teams;

5.4. Having managers lead with intend.

What Actually Happened?

1. Energizing People:

   1.1. The salary formula was received with enthusiasm by all staff;

   1.2. The merit money scheme was more than enthusiastically received and increased both the extrinsic and intrinsic motivation among the staff;

   1.3. Although some staff were hesitant at first, the personal map activities did sow the seeds for an atmosphere of trust and understanding, especially top-down;

   1.4. Knowing their staff's motivational priorities has made it possible for management to tweak and optimize the workplace;

   1.5. After a couple of iterations, the WYSIWYG Kudos Wall has become a valuable feedback tool for both staff and management.

2. Improving Competence:

   2.1. The team competence matrices created for both Front and Back of House, made it clear who needed what additional training;

   2.2. Regular mini workshops facilitated by crackerjack staff are held at the café;

   2.3. The 'Obligated Annual Learning Goals' have been embraced by all staff and also improved the intrinsic motivation of most staff members;

2.4. An environment of experimentation is slowly developing, but still needs work;

2.5. The Niko-Niko Calendar has proven to be a useful evaluation tool;

2.6. The team roles to create creative tension are still quite uncomfortable for most staff and need work.

3. Making the organization ambidextrous:

3.1. The traditional hierarchy has successfully been flattened and both the Front and Back of House teams have become more cross-functional and self-organized;

3.2. With the exception of IT and Finance, all staff is expected to be fully *T-shaped*;

3.3. It has been identified that management and Back of House should focus on efficiency whereas the Front of House is all about effectivity.

4. Empowering Teams:

4.1. Both the Front and Back of House have successfully implemented Delegation Boards;

4.2. Both the Front and Back of House have implemented a 'circle of training' to assists staff career paths.

5. Aligning Constraints:

5.1. The café's *Ikigai* has been formulated;

5.2. Core values have been identified;

5.3. S.M.A.R.T. goals have been set, but with varying degrees of success;

5.4. As with the S.M.A.R.T. goals, leading with intend is happening, but with varying degrees of success.

Why Did It Happen?

Because most of the practices we implemented simply at the café worked as intended, I want to focus only on those that didn't go as I expected.

1.3 *Personal Maps* — After a rocky start, in the end, the personal maps proved to be an effective tool. The reason why staff hesitated at first, I think, was because of 'face'. 'Saving face' is such a strong motivating force in Chinese culture, it might have inhibited staff from sharing the stories that shaped them into who they are today.[115]

The reason the tool worked out in the end has a lot to do with the courageous opening up of Chef Pierre who, as a senior staff member, was more than willing to share personal stories about himself.

1.5 WYSIWYG *Kudos Wall* — The Kudos Wall needed a couple of iterations to become successful. The whole process and reasoning behind this has already been described in detail in chapter two of this book.

2.4 *Running Experiments* — The Mezzanine has successfully run quite a few experiments, but the deal breaker for the other departments has been that the service industry doesn't really lend itself for experiments. Few customers would appreciate their orders being messed up because of some experiment in the kitchen. There are, however, other options and the teams are working on them.

2.6 *Team Roles* — Hong Kong's societal structure is traditionally extremely hierarchical so, in combination with the previously mentioned concept of 'face' this makes it hard for younger staff to 'play' roles like challenger or executor. But it's work in progress.

5.3 *S.M.A.R.T. Goals* — As described in chapter five, not all staff see the point of setting S.M.A.R.T. goals for standardized work. But there's no real objection either, so it's more work in progress.

5.4 Leading with Intent — As above, work in progress.

What Did We Learn from It?

Looking at the "What actually happened?" and "Why did it happen?" sections above, I think we can conclude that many of the Management 3.0 practices can easily be implemented in any organization and that the aim of making one's employees happier is very much within reach.

However, some practices are more culturally sensitive and might need to be adjusted or given longer time to be implemented successfully.

The Celebration Grid

A Management 3.0 tool we haven't discussed yet is the so-called *celebration grid* (aka experimentation matrix). According to Management 3.0 thinker and practitioner Jurgen Appelo, the grid is a visual representation of ideas outlined in Donald G. Reinertsen's notoriously dry and complicated book *The principles of Product Development Flow*.[116]

The celebration grid makes it almost child's play for managers to identify and discuss behaviours versus outcomes and success versus failure. Simply put, the grid (figure 27), is divided into columns: Mistakes, Experiments and Practices, and categories: Success, Failure and Learning.

The Practices column is the most straightforward, if you do the right things the right way, you'll likely be successful. Sadly enough, even the best tried-and-tested practises fail every now and then. But this is not necessarily a reflection on the team that failed. As long as they reflect on what happened, they will learn and avoid failure in the future.

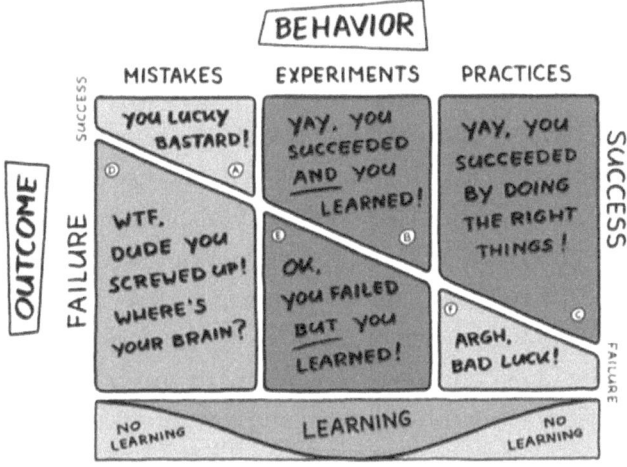

Figure 27: Celebration Grid © Jurgen Appelo

One example of a best practice that might fail is the use of checklists. The thinking behind checklists is hard to argue against as a good checklist breaks down a complicated procedure into a series of logical, easy to follow, steps. But what if something happens that isn't covered by the checklist? Everything we do and use today is far more complex than it used to be, so unless checklists are continually evaluated and updated, they might end up doing more harm than good.

More interesting I find the Mistakes column. Mistakes tend to lead to failure, but sometimes something gone wrong can actually lead to success. And as long as we reflect on and try to understand our failures, we will learn from them and possibly be successful at a later time. A well-known example of this is the Post-it Note. Back in 1968, a 3M research scientist attempted to create a super strong glue, but he failed. Then in 1974, one of his colleagues found that the failed glue had an interesting characteristic, a strip of paper with the unglue swiped onto its edges could be stuck on any surface and stay in place. When not needed anymore, it could be easily removed without any harm done. The idea of an improved bookmark was born and Post-it Notes rapidly became the top-selling office-supply they are today.[117]

The most interesting column to me is Experiments. In this column both success and failure are equal (i.e. successful). Why? Basically, experimenting means trying something new without knowing if the outcome will succeed or not. As we discussed in chapter two, a good experiment should fail 50% of the time.

When we put together a celebration grid at Naked Espresso, after answering the questions of the after-action review, management responded positively. It really helped them to visualize and reflect on what had happened in the past nine months and they appreciated the focus on learning over failure.

Playbook

> *"If you're not confused,*
> *you're not paying attention."*
> **~ Tom Peters**

A business playbook typically contains all the pieces and parts that make up an organization's go-to approach for getting things done. On the assumption that you will feel inspired by the case study of Naked Espresso, I've put together a 12-step playbook which you can use to lead your own organization into the realm of Management 3.0.

12 Steps towards Management 3.0

1. Form a dedicated team.

Like with any change manage effort, introducing Management 3.0 practices can't be done as a side-hustle. Form a diverse team of different stakeholders around you to help you lead the journey towards Management 3.0.

2. Define the organization's purpose and core values.

The first task of your Management 3.0 team should be to work out the 'Why' of the business *(Ikigai)* and to draft its core values.

3. **Figure out how the organization might become more ambidextrous.**

   Next you should take a thorough look at your organization's structure and work out how it could become more ambidextrous by better balancing: hierarchies vs networks; specialization vs generalization; efficiency vs effectivity and centralized vs decentralized command-control.

4. **Learn more about the intrinsic motivational factors of all staff *(i.e. from CEO to intern).***

   After steps 1-3, it's time to learn more about what makes your employees tick. The most straightforward way to do this is by means of *personal maps* and the *CHAMPFROGS moving motivators* game.

5. **Formulate clear mission and vision statements.**

   You should rewrite your organization's mission and vision statements for external use to reflect the change towards the new paradigm but, more importantly, you should write statements for internal use to help guide staff through the change process.

6. **Devise a transparent salary formula.**

   A good *salary formula* enhances transparency and allows employees to understand their full earning potential, what they need to do to achieve it and empowers them to define their own professional development path.

If applicable to the kind of business you're in, you should also try to come up with a creative *merit money scheme.*

7. Complete competence matrices for the teams.

Have each of your teams fill out a *competence matrix* to obtain a clear picture of their strengths and weaknesses before trying to make them more competent.

8. Develop individual and team training paths.

You should work out who needs what kind of training and how you can encourage (and enable) self-study. The ultimate goal here is to have your teams become cross-functional and self-organized and your employees *T-shaped*.

9. Train for trust.

To be able to delegate your responsibilities, you need to be sure your staff will do the work assigned to them the way you expect them to do it and that the result will be what you were aiming for. To achieve this, you need to train for trust.

10. Forge creative tension within teams

Assign roles such as *coordinator, challenger* and *thinker* to team members, this will help them challenge each other which in turn will heighten the creative tension. Crucial here is that the roles assigned are clearly outlined and that everyone understands the function of different roles. If this is not the case roleplay might lead to negative creative tension.

11. Establish rituals.

Rituals are habit forming and thus play an important role in creating your organizational culture. The kind of ritual, early morning briefings or Friday afternoon Happy Hour, doesn't matter as long as they are consistent.

12. Set-up delegation boards.

Delegation boards create openness and transparency of expectations between managers and their teams. If managers and their teams create these boards together and prominently display them, everyone knows who can do what. The boards will empower the teams and free up valuable time for the managers.

Of course, these twelve steps are just the beginning. As mentioned numerous times before, Management 3.0 isn't a framework you can just copy-paste into the organization. It's an ongoing process of discussions and experimentation, trial and error. But the steps in this little playbook (which do not necessarily need to be taken in this order, by the way) will get you going. Give it a try and find out how your business might benefit from the next iteration of management.

Bonus Chapter

Wu-Wei & MGT 3.0

> *"A leader is best when his people barely
> know he exists, when his work is done, his
> aim fulfilled, they will say they did it themselves."*
> **~ Laozi**

I facilitate Management 3.0 workshops all over the
Asia-Pacific region on behalf of the Wu-Wei Research Institute, a Hong Kong-based think tank
concerned with researching disconcerting questions about the ontological Self and sustainable living in contemporary urban society.

Hong Kong, the location in which I set this case
study, is probably one of the least likely places on
this planet to embrace Management 3.0 practices.

Corporate culture in the former British Crown
Colony is still almost 19th century hierarchical,
with some larger organizations having up to 50
echelons in their chain of command, and the job title reigns supreme. It dictates where your desk will
be, which elevators and toilets you can use, where
and how long you can have lunch, and even who
you can and can't talk to both up and down the line.
To be at the bottom of the pyramid in Hong Kong
is tough. As one dock worker puts it, "I think people

in Hong Kong work under great pressure, with long working hours but short holidays. I think Hong Kong is a good travel destination but it's not a good place to live in."[118]

However, despite its antiquated British heritage, Hong Kong is also a profoundly Chinese society and its local culture is deeply influenced by Confucian and Daoist philosophies, as well as the traditional practice of *feng shui*.* It is for this reason that I would like to share with you this bonus chapter on the ancient Daoist concept of *wu-wei* and the philosophical merit it might bring to Management 3.0. But before we get into that, let's have a look at what wu-wei actually is.

What is Wu-Wei?

Literally translated, the traditional Chinese logograms 無 (*wú*) and 爲 (*wéi*) mean 'doing nothing', but as a philosophical concept it better translates as 'doing without trying' or 'effortless action'. You could compare this to 'being in the zone' or achieving a 'state of flow'. [119]

My first introduction to this ancient Chinese concept was when I read about it in de *Daodejing* which is a fundamental text for both philosophical and religious Daoism that has inspired

---

* *Feng shui* is an ancient Chinese practice, which claims to use invisible energy forces *(qi)* to harmonize individuals with their surrounding environment. In Hong Kong, Feng shui is often used to orient buildings in an auspicious manner.

philosophers, poets, painters, even cooks and gardeners since it was written more than 2,500 years ago by the largely mythical figure of Laozi. [120]

Laozi is normally represented as one man but most scholars today believe the book is actually the work of a number of authors, collectively referred to as the Old Masters: *the Laozi*.

I'd like to give you four examples to show you what wu-wei entails. Two have been taken from Laozi's *Daodejing* and the other two have been inspired by the philosophies of Chinese sages Confucius and Zhuangzi, who both lived a couple of centuries BCE.[121]

First Confucius, arguably the most famous Chinese thinker. Confucianism is all about morality and the correct practise of rituals and so not surprisingly, he compares wu-wei to the carving and polishing of the Self. What he means by this is that if you try something new and then practice it continuously, over time you will internalise and embody the process. You'll achieve wu-wei.

I think the clearest example of this is learning how to drive a stick-shift car. If you learnt this, I'm sure you remember how difficult it was at first. You checked your mirrors, applied the brake, pressed down the clutch pedal, shifted gear, let the clutch come up slowly and then... gas, but not too much. Difficult wasn't it?

I'll bet that, like me, you also stalled the engine more than one and got scolded for shifting gears too early or too late. But once you mastered the basics, the whole experience changed completely. Now, instead of over-thinking, sweating and changing your mind in the middle of an action, you shift gears without a single conscious thought, that is wu-wei.

My second example comes from the approach to wu-wei in the *Daodejing*. Laozi is far more radical than Confucius and claims we should never even try to achieve wu-wei. Instead of learning and practising, we should just forget about it and rely on the *Dao*, the Universe, to make things happen.

An example of this I can personally relate to is that of travel. On the one hand you could spend weeks planning all the details of your trip: book the hotels, get insured and even write a day-to-day itinerary. But, on the other hand, you could just look for a cheap ticket to any visa-free destination, pack a carry-on bag, grab your passport and leave. When you get to your destination, you should make sure you get lost and see what happens. From personal experience I can tell you that this latter option leads to far more interesting trips. It's the quintessential wu-wei of travel.

Another example of Laozi's wu-wei takes us back to my days as a sergeant with the Royal Horse Artillery. As a group commander of 12 soldiers, I had a reputation of being a sympathetic listener. That surprised me as I did not see myself like that at all. I thought long and hard about it, why would they think that? Then, I realised that I wasn't that compassionate at all, but I did let people speak. In the army soldiers always hear they should shut up and do as they're told. I never liked that when my superiors did that to me and so, unknowingly I should admit, I followed the Confucian Golden Rule, "What you do not wish for yourself, do not do to others."[122] I'd let my soldiers whine and complain until they felt they'd said it all. They had their say and went back to work. In other words, by me doing nothing, nothing was left undone.* As a result, I had the best functioning group in the unit. That also is wu-wei.

My last example comes from Zhuangzi, a Daoist sceptic philosopher. He disagrees with both Confucius and Laozi and says we shouldn't try and we should not, not try. We should just go with the flow and ride the wave. Like Michelangelo, we should not think about how to carve a sculpture but simply look at a block of marble, discover the statue locked inside and set it free.

From a personal perspective, I can tell you that I reached Zhuangzi's sense of wu-wei in October 2016. I'd always wanted to be a writer and like so many others, I'd started a bunch of books but never finished any of them. To actually go from "It was a dark stormy night," to a resounding "the end," seemed an impossible task.

Then, in the summer of 2015, I was asked to write some short stories for a website. I took on the challenge and enjoyed the pressure of a weekly

---

* "When nothing is done, nothing is left undone." is a famous quote from the *Daodejing* (Verse 37).

deadline. After about a year of doing this, I realized that I had enough material for an actual book. So by not trying to write a book and not, not trying to write one, I had finally written my book.[123]

This really sums up what wu-wei means to me: To thoroughly practice the things worth learning, to often explore the unknown and, most of all, to always ride the waves of opportunity. That is wu-wei, but what has all of that to do with Management 3.0, you might be wondering?

Effortless Action in Management 3.0

In one of his State of the Union addresses, US President Ronald Reagan quoted the previously mentioned Chinese philosopher Laozi who once said, "Govern a great nation as you would cook a small fish; do not overdo it."[124] I would argue that the same goes for successfully managing a business in today's creative economy.

Management 3.0 aims to do just that, have managers perfectly cook a small fish. The teams are the fish and their work environment is the pan. Once the pan is heated and the fish is laid into the oil, the cook only needs to give the pan a quick shake every now and then and maybe turn the fish over once; everything else will take care of itself.

Likewise, all a manager needs to do is to create an optimized work environment (heat and oil the pan), introduce the team to the objective they have to meet (place the fish in the pan) and then let them get on with the task. Under management 3.0, the manager only needs to check-in with the team (shake the pan) sporadically. This is why I think Management 3.0 is a very Daoist theory and its aim to make management a group responsibility is very much in line with wu-wei. Probably without realizing it, management theorist Jurgen Appelo has taken us back to the wisdom of the ancient sages. And that's a good thing because, in the words of the sage Confucius you should, "study the past if you want to define the future."

To move towards (or back to, depending on how you look at it) Management 3.0 can be unnerving and challenging, but I hope this book has inspired you to give it a try. If you do, keep in mind this final quote from the *Daodejing:*

"Do you have the patience to wait till
your mud settles and the water is clear?
Can you remain unmoving till the
right action arises by itself?"
(*Daodejing*, Verse 15)

[T]here you are.

Further Readings

Management 3.0 isn't a new framework, nor a new set of ideas. Instead it is a set of practices based on a distillation of the ideas most contemporary management and leadership books have in common and agree upon.

To work out better what might work best for your own organization, I'd highly recommend the following reading list which contains most of the books Management 3.0 theory is based upon. I've listed them by title, because I feel the books themselves are more important than their authors.

Accelerate – John P. Kotter
Adapt – Tim Harford
Adaptive Action – Glenda H. Eoyang
Behind Closed Doors – J. Rothman, E. Derby
Coherence in the Midst of Complexity – Hugo Letiche
Complexity and Organizational Reality – Ralph D. Stacey
Conscious Capitalism – John Mackey
Creative Confidence – Tom Kelley & David Kelley
Drive – Daniel H. Pink
Freedom from Command & Control – John Seddon
Hire with Your Head – Lou Adler
How Google Works – Eric Schmidt

Humble Inquiry – Edgar H. Schein

Lean Enterprise – Jez Humble, et al.

Like a Virgin – Richard Branson

Management – Peter F. Drucker

Management 3.0 – Jurgen Appelo

Management: Revised Edition – Peter F. Drucker

Managing – Henry Mintzberg

Managing for Happiness – Jurgen Appelo

Motivation and Personality – Abraham Maslow

Organizational Design - Richard M. Burton, et al.

Principles of Prod. Dev. Flow – Donald G. Reinertsen

Radical Management – Stephen Denning

Reinventing Organizations – Frédéric Laloux

Self-Determination Research – Ryan Deci

Simply Managing – Henry Mintzberg

SMART & Gets Things Done – Joel Spolsky

The Advantage – Patrick Lencioni

The Ambidextrous Organization – Jens Maier

The Art of Powerful Questions – Eric E. Vogt, et al.

The Connected Company – Dave Gray

The Fifth Discipline – Peter M. Senge

The Interaction of Compl. and Mgmt – Michael Lissack

The Lean Startup – Eric Ries

The Modern Firm – John Roberts

The Motivation to Work – Frederick Herzberg

The Systems View of Life – Fritjof Capra

Time to Think – Nancy Kline

What Matters Now – Gary Hamel

Who Am I? – Steven Reiss

Work Rules! – Laszlo Bock

References

[1] Management 3.0 (n.d.) *Case Studies*. Management 3.0: https://buff.ly/2ZcjR5u

[2] Maximini, D. (2018) *Agile Leadership in Practice: Applying Management 3.0.* Norderstedt, Germany: BoD.

[3] Minford, J. (Ed.) (2003) *The Art of War.* New York, NY: Penguin Classics.

[4] Wren, D. A. (2005) *The History of Management Thought* (5th ed.) Chichester, UK: John Wiley & Sons.

[5] Plato, & Reeve, C. D. (2004) *Republic* (1st ed.) Indianapolis, IN: Hackett Publishing Company.

[6] Wren, D. A. (2005) *The History of Management Thought* (5th ed.) Chichester, UK: John Wiley & Sons.

[7] Wren, D. A. (2005) *The History of Management Thought* (5th ed.) Chichester, UK: John Wiley & Sons.

[8] Kautilya. (1915) *Arthaśāstra.* Wikisource.org: https://buff.ly/2ZaGXJz

[9] ZA Blog (2018) *The Nicene Creed: Where it came from and why it still matters*. Zondervan Academic: https://buff.ly/3bGiv5i

10   Wren, D. A. (2005) *The History of Management Thought* (5th ed.) Chichester, UK: John Wiley & Sons.

11   Bissell, R. E., Sciabarra, C. M., & Younkins, E. W. (Eds.) (2019) *The Dialectics of Liberty: Exploring the Context of Human Freedom.* Lanham, MD: Lexington Books.

12   Rosenthal, C. (2013, March) *Big Data In The Age Of The Telegraph*. McKinsey Quarterly.

13   UShistory.org. (n.d.) *The New Tycoons: Andrew Carnegie*. US History: https://buff.ly/2z3KDlL

14   Fayol, H. (2013) *General and Industrial Management.* Eastford, CT: Martino Fine Books.

15   Mind Tools (2018) *Henri Fayol's Principles of Management.* Mind Tools: https://buff.ly/2yaab0b

16   Fayol, H. (2013) *General and Industrial Management.* Eastford, CT: Martino Fine Books.

17   Taylor, F. W. (1997). *The Principles Of Scientific Management.* Mineola, NY: Dover Publications.

18 Akrani, G. (2011) *Frederick Taylor's Principles of Scientific Management Theory*. Kalyan City Life: https://buff.ly/2A9RQkF.

19   Fayol, H. (2013) *General and Industrial Management.* Eastford, CT: Martino Fine Books.

20   Business Dictionary (n.d.). *Fordism.* Business Dictionary: https://buff.ly/366Md2b

[21] Tranter, L. (2018) *The History And Future Of Management*. Extreme Uncertainty: https://buff.ly/2p8Jzoi

[22] Tranter, L. (2018) *The History And Future Of Management*. Extreme Uncertainty: https://buff.ly/2p8Jzoi

[23] Do, D. (n.d.) *What is Muda, Mura, and Muri?* The Lean Way: https://buff.ly/2UwCRX1

[24] Liker, J. K. (2004) *The Toyota Way - 14 Management Priciples From The World's Greatest Manudacturer.* New York, NY: McGraw-Hill.

[25] Tranter, L. (2018) *The History And Future Of Management*. Extreme Uncertainty: https://buff.ly/2p8Jzoi

[26] Tranter, L. (2015) *Difference between Agile and Lean*. Extreme Uncertainty: https://buff.ly/2IeXnFX

[27] Senge, P. M. (2006) *The Fifth Discipline: The Art & Practice of The Learning Organization.* New York, NY: Doubleday.

[28] Tranter, L. (2018) *The History And Future Of Management*. Extreme Uncertainty: https://buff.ly/2p8Jzoi

[29] Tranter, L. (2018) *The History And Future Of Management*. Extreme Uncertainty: https://buff.ly/2p8Jzoi

30 Appelo, J. (2010) *Management 3.0: Leading Agile Developers, Developing Agile Leaders.* Boston, MA: Addison-Wesley.

31 Appelo, J. (2016) *Managing for Happiness: Games, Tools, and Practices to Motivate Any Team.* Hoboken, NJ: John Wiley & Sons.

32 Aaslaid, K. (2018) *50 Examples of Corporations that Failed to Innovate.* Valuer: https://buff.ly/3dTmXzf

33 Ross, H. J., & Tartaglione, J. R. (2018) *Our Search for Belonging: How Our Need to Connect Is Tearing Us Apart.* Oakland, CA: Berett-Koehler Publisheres, Inc.

34 Appelo, J. (2010) *Management 3.0: Leading Agile Developers, Developing Agile Leaders.* Boston, MA: Addison-Wesley.

35 Bauch, D. (2005) *Swindon Magic Roundabout* [Online image] Wikimedia Commons: https://buff.ly/3fUtqM9

36 Marschall, A. (2008) *The Brilliant Sorcery of England's 7-Circle Magic Roundabout*. Wired: https://buff.ly/3dS4wuJ

37 Marschall, A. (2008) *The Brilliant Sorcery of England's 7-Circle Magic Roundabout*. Wired: https://buff.ly/3dS4wuJ

38 Snowden, D. [Ohio State Wexner MC] (2012) *Combining Complexity Theory with Narrative Research* [Video] Youtube: https://buff.ly/2LBSWlc

[39] Appelo, J. (2011) *Management 3.0 – Complexity Thinking.* [Slide deck] Slideshare: https://buff.ly/2LAzMCu

[40] Thoreau, H. D. (2004) *Walden* (150th Anniversary Edition). Princeton, NJ: Princeton University Press.

[41] Graham, D. A. (2014) *Rumsfeld's Knowns and Unknowns: The Intellectual History of a Quip.* The Atlantic: https://buff.ly/2kM8mMG

[42] Žižek, S. (2008) *Rumsfeld and the bees.* The Guardian: https://buff.ly/364aKVR

[43] Oswald, D. (2013) *Admitting You Have a Problem Is the First Step in Fixing the Problem.* HR Daily Advisor: https://buff.ly/3bC5JFa

[44] Lissack, M. R. (Ed.) (2002) *The Interaction of Complexity and Management.* Santa Barbara, CA: Preager Publishers.

[45] Stacey, R. D. (2010) *Complexity and Organizational Reality.* (2nd ed.). London, UK: Routledge.

[46] Rother, M. (2009) *Toyota Kata: Managing People for Improvement, Adaptiveness and Superior Results.* (1st ed.). New York, NY: McGraw-Hill Education.

[47] Ries, R. (2011) *The Lean Startup.* (1st ed.). Redfern, NSW: Currency Press.

48 Appelo, J. (2010) *Management 3.0: Leading Agile Developers, Developing Agile Leaders.* Boston, MA: Addison-Wesley.

49 Pressman, E. R. [Producer] & Stone, O. [Director] (1987) *Wall Street.* [Film] 20th Century Fox.

50 Appelo, J. (2016) *Managing for Happiness: Games, Tools, and Practices to Motivate Any Team.* Hoboken, NJ: John Wiley & Sons.

51 Sinek, S. [Simon Sinek] (2016) *The Millennial Question.* [Video] Youtube: https://buff.ly/3bBW01l

52 Peters, T. J. and Waterman, R. H. (2006) *In Search of Excellence.* New York, NY: HarperCollins Publishers.

53 Appelo, J. (2016) *Managing for Happiness: Games, Tools, and Practices to Motivate Any Team.* Hoboken, NJ: John Wiley & Sons.

54 Appelo, J. (2016) *Managing for Happiness: Games, Tools, and Practices to Motivate Any Team.* Hoboken, NJ: John Wiley & Sons.

55 Appelo, J. (2016) *Managing for Happiness: Games, Tools, and Practices to Motivate Any Team.* Hoboken, NJ: John Wiley & Sons.

56 Eifler, A. (2013) *A Team is only as Strong as its Weakest Player.* Andrew Eifler: https://buff.ly/368OzgY

57 TEG Coaching (2008) *Positive Quotes.* Coach Annette: https://buff.ly/2WHNie5

58 Morrison, J. E. and Meliza, L. L. (1999) *Foundations of the After Action Review Process* [PDF File]. Institute for Defence Analyses. https://buff.ly/36BNcHU

59 Branson, R. [Big Think] (2011) *Advice for Entrepreneurs.* [Video] Youtube: https://buff.ly/2JzYwZh

60 Appelo, J. (2016). *Managing for Happiness: Games, Tools, and Practices to Motivate Any Team.* Hoboken, NJ: John Wiley & Sons.

61 Eby, K. (2016) *Comprehensive Guide to the Agile Manifesto.* Smartsheet: https://buff.ly/2Zf4SaL

62 Johnson, S. (2010) *Where Good Ideas Come From.* (1st ed.) New York, NY: Riverhead Books.

63 Johnson, S. (2010) *Where Good Ideas Come From.* (1st ed.) New York, NY: Riverhead Books.

64 Drucker, P. F. (2008) *Management* Revised Edition. New York, NY: HarperCollins Publishers.

65 Burton, R. M., Obel, B. & DeSanctis, G. (2011) *Organizational Design: A Step-by-Step Approach.* (2nd ed.) Cambridge, UK: Cambridge University Press.

66 Burton, R. M., Obel, B. & DeSanctis, G. (2011) *Organizational Design: A Step-by-Step Approach.* (2nd ed.) Cambridge, UK: Cambridge University Press.

[67] Roberts, J. (2007) *The Modern Firm.* Cambridge, UK: Cambridge University Press.

[68] Harford, T. (2012) *Adapt: Why Success Always Starts with Failure*. London, UK: Picador.

[69] Bogsnes, B. (2016) *Implementing Beyond Budgeting: Unlocking the Performance Potential.* Hoboken, NJ: John Wiley & Sons.

[70] Kotter, J. P. (2014) *Accelerate: Building Strategic Agility for a Faster-Moving World.* (1st ed.) Brighton, MA: Harvard Business Review Press.

[71] Thomson, L. L. (2007) *Making the Team* (3rd Ed.) Upper Saddle River, NJ: Prentice Hall.

[72] Porter, M. E. (2004) *Competitive Advantage: Creating and Sustaining Superior Performance.* New York, NY: Free Press.

[73] Morgan, J. (2014) *The Future of Work.* Hoboken, NJ: John Wiley & Sons.

[74] McGreal, D. (2014) *Development Team Size.* Scrum.org: https://buff.ly/2TcCX7r

[75] Burkus, D. (2016) *Write, Then Keep Rewriting Your Org Chart.* Forbes: https://buff.ly/2ZcmsMM

[76] Ikerd, J. (2005) *Sustainable Capitalism: A Matter of Common Sense.* West Hartford, CT: Kumarian Press.

[77] Church, M. O. (2012) *What Is Open Allocation*? Forbes: https://buff.ly/2Lz6fsR

[78] McChrystal, S., Collins, T., Silverman, D. & Fussell, C. (2015) *Team of Teams: New Rules of Engagement for a Complex World*. New York, NY: Portfolio Books.

[79] Pack, M. M. (2002) *How It All Began: A Brief History of the Kitchen Brigade.* Austin Chronicle: https://buff.ly/365Dq0F

[80] Aaron, R. (2008) *Double Your Income Doing What You Love.* Hoboken, NJ: John Wiley & Sons.

[81] Management 3.0 (2019) *Delegation and Empowerment: The Seven Levels of Delegation.* [Slide deck] SlideShare: https://buff.ly/2Za5Dln

[82] Mintzberg, H. (2013) *Simply Managing: What Managers Do - and Can Do Better.* Philadelphia, PA: Trans-Atlantic Publications.

[83] Appelo, J. (2016) *Managing for Happiness: Games, Tools, and Practices to Motivate Any Team*. Hoboken, NJ: John Wiley & Sons.

[84] Appelo, J. (2016) *Managing for Happiness: Games, Tools, and Practices to Motivate Any Team.* Hoboken, NJ: John Wiley & Sons.

[85] Ackhoff, R. L. (1999) *Re-Creating the Corporation: A Design of Organizations for the 21st Century.* (1st. Ed.). Oxford, UK: Oxford University Press.

86 Management 3.0 (2019) *Delegation and Empowerment: The Seven Levels of Delegation.* [Slide deck].
SlideShare: https://buff.ly/2Za5Dln

87 Appelo, J. (2016) *Managing for Happiness: Games,
Tools, and Practices to Motivate Any Team.* Hoboken,
NJ: John Wiley & Sons.

88 Appelo, J. (2016) *Managing for Happiness: Games,
Tools, and Practices to Motivate Any Team.* Hoboken,
NJ: John Wiley & Sons.

89 Management 3.0 (2019) *Delegation and Empowerment: The Seven Levels of Delegation.* [Slide deck].
SlideShare: https://buff.ly/2Za5Dln

90 Maxwell, J. [P PG] (2013) *The 5 Levels of Leadership.*
[Video] Youtube: https://buff.ly/3673Izo

91 Charnas. D. (2016) *Work Clean.* Emmaus, PA: Rodale
Books

92 Feloni, R. (2015) *Former Navy SEAL commander explains the philosophy that made his unit the most dec-
orated of the Iraq War.* Business Insider:
https://buff.ly/3elbDfn

93 Overdeem, B. (2015) *Henrik Kniberg – Alignment vs Au-
tonomy.* Barry Overdeem: https://buff.ly/2yTtKKB

94 Mackey, J. (2014) *Conscious Capitalism: Liberating the
Heroic Spirit of Business.* Brighton, MA: Harvard Business Review Press.

95 Lencioni, P. (2012) *The Advantage: Why Organizational Health Trumps Everything Else In Business.* San Francisco, CA: Josey-Bass Books.

96 Solomon, L. (2015) *The Top Complaints from Employees About Their Leaders.* Harvard Business Review: https://buff.ly/1M5RsRG

97 Sinek, S. [TEDx Talks] (2009) *Start With Why: How Great Leaders Inspire Action.* [Video] Youtube: https://buff.ly/18W43FC

98 Jobs, S. [SteveJobsVideo] (2012) *2001 First iPod Introduction - Steve Jobs Keynote.* [Video] Youtube: https://buff.ly/3by9sU8

99 Della, J. (2018) *Ikigai for Business* [Kindle version]

100 Fried, J. and Heinemeier Hanson, D. (2010) *Rework.* Redfern, NSW: Currency Press.

101 Management 3.0 (2019) *Values & Culture.* [Slide deck]. SlideShare: https://buff.ly/2TdULzd

102 Management 3.0 (2019) *Values & Culture.* [Slide deck]. SlideShare: https://buff.ly/2TdULzd

103 Management 3.0 (n.d.) Culture Books. Management 3.0: https://buff.ly/2TzDyys

104 Galbraith, J. R. (2000) *Designing the Global Corporation* (1st ed.). San Francisco, CA: Jossey-Bass Books.

105 Darling, M., Parry, C. & Moore, J. (2005) *Learning in the Thick of It.* Harvard Business Review: https://buff.ly/2Z2QrD7

106 Catmull, E. E. and Wallace, A. (2014) Creativity, Inc. *Overcoming the Unseen Forces That Stand in the Way of True Inspiration.* London, UK: Transworld Publishers.

107 Wu-Wei Research Institute (2020) *Management 3.0 – Improving Everything.* [Slide deck] Slideshare: https://buff.ly/3669SQt

108 Loebecke, C., Van Fenema, P. & Powell, P. (1999). *Coopetition and Knowledge Transfer.* ACM SIGMIS Database. 30 (2): 14–25. doi:10.1145/383371.383373

109 Wu-Wei Research Institute (2020) *Management 3.0 – Improving Everything.* [Slide deck] Slideshare: https://buff.ly/3669SQt

110 Wu-Wei Research Institute (2020) *Management 3.0 – Improving Everything.* [Slide deck] Slideshare: https://buff.ly/3669SQt

111 Lakhiane, V. [Life At Mindvalley] (2014) *How To Transform Your Company Culture And Attract Brilliant Talent.* [Video] Youtube: https://buff.ly/1Abwq9r

112 McKinsey [McKinseyLD] (2014) *McKinsey on Change Management.* [Video] Youtube: https://buff.ly/2ZcWmcy

[113] Kotter, J. P. (1996). *Leading Change.* Boston, MA: Harvard Business School Press.

[114] Darling, M., Parry, C. & Moore, J. (2005) *Learning in the Thick of It.* Harvard Business Review: https://buff.ly/2Z2QrD7

[115] China Mike (2020) *The Cult of "Face" in China* | 面子. China Mike: https://buff.ly/2TiAxo5

[116] Reinertsen, D. G. (2009) *The Principles of Product Development Flow.* Redondo Beach, CA: Celeritas

[117] Bellis, M. (2019) *Invention of the Post-It Note*. ThoughtCo: https://buff.ly/2zJaWh4

[118] The Layover S01E05 (2011) *Hong Kong.* [TV Show] Travel Channel.

[119] Slingerland, E. (2003) *Effortless Action: Wu-Wei as Conceptual Metaphor and Spiritual Ideal in Early China*. New York, NY: Oxford University Press.

[120] Ames, R. T. & Hall, D. L. (2004) *Daodejing: A Philosophical Translation.* New York, NY: Ballantine Books

[121] Gaans, M. van [Wu-Wei Research Institute] (2017) *Trying Not to Try | PechaKucha Night, Vientiane, Laos.* [Video] Youtube: https://buff.ly/36PTbI3

[122] Legge, J. (2011) *Confucianism, The Analects, Wei Ling Gong.* Chinese Text Project: https://buff.ly/2TJp4hr

[123] Gaans, M. van (2016) *In the Moment: A Disjointed Audiobiography.* Hong Kong: Wu-Wei Institute Press.

[124] Boaz, D. (2015) *Govern a Great Country as You Would Cook a Small Fish.* CATO Institute: https://buff.ly/3blmPB8

About the Author

LIKE YOU, ontological leadership expert, philosopher and teacher Marko van Gaans has always wondered about the definition of the word leadership. Is it a noun or a verb? Is it about charisma and decisive action? Pinstripe suits and power ties? Is it just meant for the happy few, or is there a whole different narrative?

Having spent eight years as a Non-Commissioned Officer in the Royal Netherlands Army, been an educator for over two decades and, most importantly, with almost half a century of in-the-trenches life experience, Marko looks at the world differently. He appreciates, and shares with you, that leadership really is a state of being and not about the title or position. Leadership is for everyone, every day; it's how we should live our lives.

Presently, Marko serves as Philosopher-in-Residence, Workshop Facilitator and Principal Analyst at the Wu-Wei Research Institute, a Hong Kong based think tank concerned with researching disconcerting questions about the ontological Self and sustainable living in contemporary urban society.

Prior to this current position, Marko, a philosopher and human geographer by education and passion, trained senior NATO officers in computer simulated war games and taught, among many others, government officials in Laos.

wuwei-inst.org/philosopher-in-residence/